CW0070428O

GOLLANCZ, 1995

Up and Down
FIVE STAR, 2000

The Best of Round the Horne
WITH BARRY TOOK; BOXTREE, 2000

In and Out
FIVE STAR, 2001

Twenty Seventeen
HEINEMANN, 2002

Do the World a Favour and Other Stories
FIVE STAR, 2003

The Pocket Essential Classic Radio Comedy
POCKET ESSENTIALS, 2003

Success . . . and how to avoid it

Success . . . and how to avoid it
by Mat Coward

with cartoons by Rob Kirbyson

PUBLISHER   First published 2004 by TTA Press
5 Martins Lane, Witcham, Ely, Cambs CB6 2LB, England
www.ttapress.com

ISBN   ISBN 0 9526947 9 4

RIGHTS   *Success And How To Avoid It* © 2004 Mat Coward
Cartoons © 2004 Rob Kirbyson
Front Cover Art and Design © 2004 Edward Noon

The right of Mat Coward to be identified as the author of this work has been asserted by him in accordance with the Copyright, Designs and Patents Act 1988

All rights reserved. No part of this publicationmay be reproduced, stored in or introduced into a retrieval system, or transmitted, in any form, or by any means (electronic, mechanical, photocopying, recording or otherwise) without the prior written permission of the publisher. Any person who does any unauthorised act in relation to this publication may be liable to criminal prosecution and civil claims for damages

RECORD   A CIP catalogue record for this book is available from the British Library

This book is sold subject to the condition that it shall not by way of trade or otherwise, be lent, resold, hired out or otherwise circulated without the publisher's prior written consent in any form of binding or cover other than that in which it is published and without a similar condition including this condition being imposed on the subsequent purchaser

TYPESETTING   Designed and typeset by TTA Press

PRINTING   Printed and bound in Great Britain by Burlington Press Ltd *to G.*

3: EDITORS AND OTHER ENEMIES

4: BAD ADVICE AND WHERE TO FIND IT

5: 22 THINGS YOU ALREADY KNEW

Introduction

INTRODUCTION (SHORT)

I don't believe anyone really reads introductions, so why waste paper? I'll keep this brief.

This is not a HowToWrite book. There are plenty of those in print already. This is, instead, a book about being a freelance writer. It's a personal book – inevitably, given the nature of the writing trade – and it is an attempt to discuss the life of the freelance with a greater degree of honesty than is usually encountered in books and magazines for writers.

HowToWrite books say 'You can do it, if only you believe in yourself and follow these simple rules'. This book says 'You might do it, but you should know from the start that there really is, as you have always suspected, an inter-galactic conspiracy of space-vampires, Freemasons, and commissioning editors dedicated to keeping you in your place'.

It is not, in other words, *How To Make A Million From The Comfort Of Your Own Lounge Without Really Trying In Three Easy Lessons*.

In fact, so confident am I of this book's unique appeal, that if, as a direct result of reading *Success And How To Avoid It*, you do indeed make a million pounds from the comfort of your own lounge without really trying, I hereby undertake to refund in full the price of the book.

No questions, no quibbles, and this does not affect your statutory rights as a consumer. Good luck.

FOREWORD BY GEORGE ORWELL

In his famous (and incidentally, delightful) essay 'Why I Write' (1946), George Orwell, after an introductory passage in which he tells a familiar story of how 'perhaps from the age of five or six, I knew that when I grew up I should be a writer', goes on to list the 'four great motives for writing'. These, he says, will exist 'in different degrees in every writer' and are as follows: sheer egoism; aesthetic enthusiasm; historical impulse; and political purpose.

Orwell's principle theme in this essay (and I would strongly urge you to read it in full, if you don't already know it) is that writers produce their best work when they combine purpose with art. Many of you, however, will have noticed that there is one obvious omission from the above list: to get paid. If this item does not appear in your personal list of 'great motives' then this is not the book for you.

My own list of the proper priorities for a freelance writer is this:

1. To make a living.

2. To make a living without killing yourself, without letting the job take over your life and screw you to death.

3. To be an honest trader. That is, not to write lies without a sufficient reason; not to kow-tow to the bosses more than you really need to; to maintain whatever degree of independence you can from the system of production; to engage in solidarity with your fellows. In other words, to behave as any other class-conscious worker.

4. And it's only when I get this far down the league table that 'writing something really good' comes in, because frankly there are more important things in a writer's life, in a human's life, than writing great stuff.

Of course, if you're an artist, then Number 4 would be at Number 1, and Numbers 1 to 3 probably wouldn't exist at all. But then, if you're an artist, you're reading the wrong book, and you have my sympathy – what a dreadful affliction!

I am not an artist. I'm a skilled worker, a freelance writer, a working man with a trade.

MY WHY

This is how I became a writer, instead of working for a living.

There was a particular fortnight in the early 1980s when I was signed off work, on the sick. As it happened, a friend of mine was in those days in the middle of a lengthy period of unemployment and was living in a bedsit just around the corner from mine.

This was autumn going into winter. My friend lived in a room which had not been decorated since the day of its conversion, many years earlier. He had virtually no furniture beyond a bed and an armchair. The heating came from a small, chatty, coin-fed gas fire. You had to sit very close to it in order to get mildly warm.

He couldn't afford much food or new clothes – hell, he could barely afford booze and fags – but there were excellent public libraries nearby, and he had a little television which, though primitive, never actually blacked out. Naturally, he couldn't afford to go out and so almost all he did was sit there in that room all day.

I spent most of that fortnight's sick leave with him, sitting by the fire, chatting, saving up my urine because I didn't want to have to go up to the next landing to the freezing lav. Occasionally, I'd wander over to gaze aimlessly out of the bay window, but I'd quickly become so cold that I'd have to scuttle back to the armchair by the fire, and we'd chat some more, play the occasional board game, smoke another cigarette, and soon I began to think . . .

This is absolutely wonderful! This is the life for me! Not having to go in to work every day: what more could anyone possibly ask for than that?

That's my *Why I Write*. It's not as impressive as Orwell's, but it's just as true, in its own way.

HOW TO DEFINE YOURSELF (NOT THAT IT MATTERS)

What you call yourself is important, but only to you. Nobody else cares or even notices. For a while I used to by-line myself 'freelance columnist' and the spellchecker on my old word-processor always changed that to 'freelance communist', which I liked. I particularly liked the idea of being a *freelance* communist, as if Old Joe Stalin might ring up on Monday and tell me he needed a dictatorship of the proletariat establishing and his usual guy had let him down, and I'd say 'Today's out, mate, Bank Holiday. Tuesday-Wednesday-Thursday I'm doing a job for the Maoists. I can fit you in maybe Friday, that any good?'.

So I call myself a freelance writer, a job title for a job that doesn't really exist. The point is, I'm not exactly a *writer*, I'm not exactly a freelance *journalist* . . . I'm a freelance writer.

When I left school I moved to London and took the first job I was offered, and stuck it for nearly a year. I was a trainee junior clerk at an American bank, and my duties included fetching people sandwiches containing items to which I knew or believed them to be allergic, and making the little girls in the computer room blush by looking at them. It was a fairly dismal job, but the people were interesting, and it gave me a rich store of writer's material, none of which I have ever used. I only owned two shirts and they were both polyester.

Then I spent seven years as a junior in public libraries. The night I got that job I bought everyone in the pub a drink. A Geordie called Keith assured me I had made a sensible career move, because he knew people who'd worked in public libraries and they all said that 'The women are absolutely knockout, man'. He was right, too. The libraries were staffed almost entirely by women with perfect bottoms, who read books and voted Labour.

The public libraries of north London in those days were exciting, full of light and life and people with plans. I loved them. People would come from all over the world to study the libraries, to see how it should be done.

All gone now, of course. I became a library assistant a couple of months after Margaret Thatcher's first election victory. The Time of Evil ruined Britain's libraries as it ruined everything else in Britain; deliberately, methodically, evil for its own sake.

When I look back on the seven years I spent library assisting, it still seems like the biggest, longest, most significant part of my life, although in strictly quantitative terms it was small and long ago. That's age for you, I suppose. I thought I was a natural at being a bookstamper, I thought I was good at it, but this was a minority opinion. In the end I got bored with working – not so much with working, as *going to work* – so in June 1986 I left the libraries and became a freelance writer instead.

Was it really that easy? Well, no, not in the sense of being *easy*. It was very hard work. For a couple of years I was doing two jobs: Libraryman during the day, and then Captain Freelance in the evenings and at weekends and on my day off. I didn't really have time for anything else except my two jobs. I lost touch with friends, I neglected my revolutionary duties, I even dropped out of the darts team for a while.

But it was easy in the sense of not being difficult. A few very lucky coincidences helped, but chiefly – and I only realise this in retrospect – my timing was perfect. In the mid-80s, British capitalism went through one of its periodic mini-booms. Artificial and unsustainable though this was, it did mean that for a few years, several of London's non-industries (advertising, financial speculation, cocaine dealing, limousine whoring) were hiring staff in large numbers. This in turn meant that the revenue available to newspapers and magazines from recruitment advertising was greater than ever before. All of a sudden, periodicals were putting on more pages, more editorial was needed to pad out the extra ads, and every third Londoner who had access to a credit card was starting up his own magazine and asking his mates to write for it.

The cyclical boom-bust nature of late-period capitalism is a well studied phenomenon. The phantom economy of the yuppie years was soon exorcised by the bell, book and candle of terminal economic decline. The collapse of communism brought about a world paper shortage. The collapse of capitalism brought about a world disposable income shortage. Your mate's magazine closed. Your mate now works for other people, and no longer lunches for four hours at a time in London West One. What did you say in 2001 to a man who was on the verge of owning a new publishing empire in 1989? You said 'Spicy beanburger and fries twice, please'.

It was the perfect time to become a freelance writer, and of course the worst time. A time of illusions is no time to make career decisions. Luckily, freelance writing is no career.

A writer is someone who makes his living writing just one thing: detective novels, TV costume dramas, royal biographies. A freelance journalist is just a journalist without a regular employer; usually, these days, a journalist who was made redundant when his former employer was taken over by a multinational.

A freelance writer is . . . well, an odd-job man. Neither a proper journalist nor a niche writer, he is someone who makes his living from words, in whatever manner he can.

In my time as a freelance, I have earned money as a poet, short story writer, broadcaster of various kinds, comedy writer for TV, radio and stand-up, comic strip scripter, book reviewer, greetings card and badge sloganeer, restaurant reviewer, book writer, gardening correspondent, newspaper feature writer, magazine columnist, indexer, and probably several other things that I have either temporarily forgotten or permanently erased from my memory with or without the benefit of therapy.

The literary odd job man. If you become a freelance writer, the shingle you hang has written upon it WORDS DONE WHILE-U-WAIT. NO JOB TOO SMALL, TOO LARGE OR TOO DEMEANING.

But if you've got any sense, you'll try for something settled in the Civil Service instead. And this book will show you why.

1: Quit now, while you're still behind

BELIEVE ME, YOU DON'T WANT TO BE A WRITER

Sailors, publicans and, of course, doctors are the people most likely to die of alcohol-related liver disease, according to a major study of occupational groups published in 1995.

Fourth come lawyers, and fifth are 'artistic and literary workers', well ahead of fishermen, soldiers, dockers, and even kitchen porters. If you're a writer, you're going to die of cirrhosis. I have just one question: where do these literary workers find the *time* to drink themselves to death?

Freelance writing is a crap way to earn a living: I think that's the medical term I'm looking for. It's not coal mining and it's not streetwalking, true, but it's still far from being a way of life conducive to sound mental or physical health. (And don't forget, while we're on the subject of healthy physiques, that most people meet their husbands, wives, boyfriends and girlfriends at work – which is difficult if you work alone.)

There are two main kinds of freelance routine, and I've done them both. When I first started, I spent a couple of years rushing around London (and, occasionally, Scotland, the South, the West and the Midlands) like a man whose arse was on fire in a land where the possessor of the only fire extinguisher had moved house without leaving a forwarding address. I never ate except on expenses or in pubs, and I drank as much as I possibly could, because it was all free, even to the stage at one point of having my skellington surgically hollowed out to make space for more booze.

I was new, and unknown, so I had to take every job I was offered. I was offered plenty, because I was good, and because I was unknown and therefore cheap (as opposed to now, when I am unknown and therefore cheap but not nearly as good). I'd do several jobs a day if necessary: record a broadcast in the West End in the morning, do a newspaper feature in some distant suburb at lunchtime, attend a meeting for something that probably wasn't going to come to anything in the afternoon and then write up whatever it was I was writing up in the evening. Then I'd have breakfast and go to bed.

Some people, it is said, 'thrive on pressure'. I suspect that those are the same people who take Uzis into burger bars, but that might just be envy on my part. The fact that I hate working, and would rather do almost anything except make an effort to earn a living, may have something to do with the way I shudder every time I think back to those days.

In any case, after a few years my work pattern changed – partly because I wanted it to, and was well enough established to make it do so, and partly because nothing lasts forever – and I entered phase two. Nowadays, I get up, have breakfast, put on my bowler hat, commute for eight seconds to my office, switch on my computer, and write. I did that today, I did that yesterday, I'll do it tomorrow. I hardly see anyone, I hardly talk to anyone, and the only exercise I get is standing up every few hours to stretch my buttock muscles and fetch a cup of tea. My shoulders ache, my neck's stiff, my head hurts, my eyes sting. I am so unused to human contact that a half hour conversation leaves my throat raw and my ears ringing. My fingers are reasonably nimble from typing and from rolling cigarettes, so I suppose I should be grateful for small mercies.

Admittedly, never going out does have its advantages. For instance, last week I lost my penknife. It had fallen out of a badly-designed trouser pocket. However, because I hadn't been further than the front gate during the previous three weeks, I knew that the knife could only be in either the house or the garden, and thus it only took me four days of searching to find it.

See?

Imagine losing your penknife when you're a long-distance commuter. Nightmare!

Whichever kind of freelancing you do, you'll end up sick in body and soul. Writing is not a natural or comfortable way to spend your time. You sure you want to do this?

DEAD OR ALIVE: IS THERE A DIFFERENCE?

I think any freelance writer looking back on his life – possibly from the vantage point of a traditional death bed scene, the kind of unlikely scene which perhaps a writer might write who had not succeeded in tying up all his plot strands in time for the end of his novel, a writer like Dickens for instance – any writer looking back over a life of writing would have to conclude that it had been a wasted life.

Writers don't live, they write. That's why they're called writers. If they lived they'd be called livers. If they did things they'd be called doers. But they don't do things, they write about things, and I'm not sure you can do both. The Texan mystery writer, Kinky Friedman, has said of his decision to become a writer, 'I began searching for a lifestyle which didn't require my presence'.

All right, I'm not saying that Henry Miller died a virgin, or that Ernest Hemingway was an agoraphobic with a terror of moths – *'Oo! Er! Beastly thing, get rid of it, please somebody get it outta here, it's going to fly into my hair I know it is!'* – but I do think that writing for a living of any sort involves so much isolation and introspection, and is so life-consuming, that it doesn't leave much time or energy or spirit for living.

Not only that, but the very act of writing about things serves to disassemble them somehow, to make them unreal. Just as if you stripped down your bike to its component parts to see how it worked, you wouldn't then be able to use it as a bicycle (I mean, yeah, OK, obviously you *would* if you put it all back together again, but that merely demonstrates the inherent limits of analogy, right?).

If you want to live an interesting life, there's only one way to do it and that is to live it. Writing is a very poor substitute. It helps obviously if you've had a life before you became a writer so that you've got something to write about, which is why most writers write about nostalgia. But if you haven't had a life, and therefore have nothing to write about, don't worry unduly; this guarantees your dreary novels will be reviewed positively in all the posh papers, because posh papers are staffed exclusively by graduates who haven't had a life and therefore don't realise you're writing about nothing, or if they do realise it, rather approve of it. (This is called 'non-genre fiction', and, contrary to popular belief, it is much more profitable than popular fiction, because it is subsidised by taxes stolen from the working classes.)

There are exceptions, of course. Some people do live and write simultaneously, but it's a trick few manage. Take me, for instance. I used to have a fine old time years ago, but once I'd become a full-time writer everything sort of stopped, and now all I do is sit in my room all day writing, and what I mostly write about is what a fine old time I used to have before I became a writer. Except for days like today, when I write about writing about what a fine old time I used to have before I became a writer. I write about how those old times were, how they weren't but I wish they were, how they were and I wish they weren't, and needless to say I write a great deal about how they weren't *quite*, but might have been.

What else have I got to write about? The last time I, for instance, worked in an office with other people was 1986. Come to think of it, it must be a few years since I've even set foot in an office.

Writers are boring people because they don't do anything. They become writers and become dull even to themselves; *especially* to themselves, since themselves are pretty much the only people they ever see.

It's clear that for most of us there is a choice to be made: write or live, live or write. If you're a gambler you could do what plenty of writers do – live and live and live and then when you're about sixty try to write it all down very quickly before you die or forget. But most writers, no less than anyone else, are safe betters. They get to about thirty and think, well, I've probably used up all my chances – I'd better get on with it now.

And so their lives end, and their writing begins.

And so if you're going to the pub tonight, have one for me, because I won't be there.

People often say that the great thing about being self-employed is that 'no two days are ever the same'. What they mean by this is that every day is worse than the one before.

If you think the working week is a drag now, just wait until you've finally achieved your ambition and become a full-time freelance. Then you will find out what the term 'full-time' really means. You might not believe me now, but it's true: one day you'll miss the day job.

Freelances don't take holidays. Not unless they are very, very rich and successful, they don't; not at Christmas, not in the summer, not even at weekends. There are no days off when you're a self-employed writer.

When you're in a nine-to-five gig, the job ends as soon as you leave the building (unless, of course, you're stupid enough to have saddled yourself with a 'career'; I'm talking about proper jobs here, not the executive nightmare). Even if you're self-employed in a more physical trade, like gardening or plumbing, there will generally be some sort of distinction

ALL JOBS ARE DAY JOBS

between earning hours and resting hours; between work and hobbies.

But writing doesn't stop when the hooter goes. Partly, that's because very few of us make enough money to afford time off. Partly, it's because various elements of the writing process can happen to you at any time, in any place, under any circumstances: ideas can occur while you're asleep, or in the bath, or on the bog, or at the dentist's. Or, indeed, asleep in the bath, or on the bog at the dentist's. Or asleep on the dentist's bog.

Partly, it's because – if you're a true freelance, rather than, say, a novelist who produces one book a year – you never really finish work, or never *know* when you've finished. Yours is not the sort of product that can be completed, polished, boxed and forgotten.

Mostly, it's because freelance writing is such an inherently insecure business, that you simply don't dare stop. Even if you're doing well this year, you've still got to plan ahead, to pile up the work for next year. Your situation can change so terrifyingly quickly: you can get sacked from a regular column, obviously, but worse than that, your editor can get sacked. There can be a change of ownership of the magazine which you depend upon to pay your rent, and suddenly all the old contributors are out: new proprietors and new editors do that routinely, for no better reason than that it is the done thing.

If you take a day off tomorrow, there might be no work the day after. Whereas if you keep going for another couple of hours tonight, you could probably get one more article roughed out, or finish tidying up another story. There's always a new market to be broken into. *There is always something else to do.*

It's not even as if you can look forward to taking it easier as you get older (I'm going to stop saying 'Unless you're very rich and successful, that is', because I take it for granted that most of us never will be). There's no company pension scheme for the freelance, because there's no company. In theory you might pay into a private scheme to make up for your lost superann – but what with? If you're making enough to buy a personal pension, then surely you're making enough that you don't need to. Meanwhile, the state pension is evaporating under the burning heat of global neoliberalism, of competitiveness and labour flexibility and other modern ways of saying 'Please die now you're no longer productive'. When you're a freelance you can forget about retirement.

You felt so superior to all the wage slaves and office stiffs, as you gaily waved them goodbye: 'I've got my redundancy cheque, now all I need is a wordprocessor, and it's *so long, suckers, see you at the book-signings!*'. But that was twenty years ago. Now, while they take up bowls and learn Welsh and frolic in the garden with their grandchildren, you're still stuck to that wordprocessor, still scribbling for your supper. That's how they'll find you on the day you die, slumped over the keyboard, suspended for eternity in the middle of an uncompleted

Always assuming, that is, that you don't become too decrepit to write. A day on the sick is one of many small luxuries the freelance sacrifices in exchange for his freedom. I remember with a nostalgia you might find hard to credit, those mornings when I awoke with a bit of a sniffle, a touch of the rumbling guts, or a slight case of the night-befores, and roused myself just long enough to phone the boss at nine, make my excuses, and stay in bed. A whole day with nothing to do but eat Disprins and listen to *Afternoon Theatre*; and, of course, look forward to a miraculously unaltered payslip. Tuesdays were favourite, as I remember; less obvious than Mondays, and it broke the week up nicely.

Not any more. When you're self-employed nobody pays you for not doing anything. This merciless rule doesn't only apply to whole days, either. Smoke-breaks in the lavs . . . that extra fifteen minutes on the lunch hour, because no one noticed what time you left . . . the late arrival and the early escape ('Sorry, boss, those trains just get worse and worse') . . . the extended, flirting loiter by the coffee machine . . . the wander along the corridors 'to deliver a message' which uses up half the morning . . . the 'popping out on an errand' which uses up half the afternoon . . . even the happy times spent staring intently at nothing, with a load of papers spread out on your desk in case anyone comes in . . .

I'll tell you something else I discovered on the day I left work for the last time: telephone calls aren't free. I know, scarcely credible, is it? But I swear it's true – turns out there's this fascist organisation known as The Phone Company which actually has the cheek, the insensitivity, the *sheer lack of good taste* to send you a bill for all the lingering chats you used to enjoy at your employer's expense, but are now forced to make from home. And they call that an enterprise culture, do they? Bastards.

While we're at it, here's another thing I bet you didn't know. You work in a stationery supermarket, a free-for-all wonderland of sellotape, staplers, envelopes and typing paper. Colleagues, note my words: until you have paid with your own cold cash for a packet of rubber bands and a printer ribbon, you just can't conceive how uncompromisingly brutal is the solo life.

HERE COME DE DOOM SACK

My heart sinks on Fridays, because I know I never get any decent post on Saturdays, or even if I do, I can't respond to it for 48 hours. The daily postal delivery dominates my life: waiting for it, anticipating it, being let down by it. A large, varied, productive post can set me up for the day; when all I get is a couple of charity circulars, a misdelivered birthday card and a credit card bill, it can cast me down for the week.

My emotional state is determined by the state of my mail. To the freelance, post is everything; all potentialities are there in the sack, until my postman, Mr Schrödinger, drops the day's catch through the flap, and the waves of possibility harden into, almost invariably, disappointment. Junk mail irritates you; it nearly kills me.

There's no post at all on Sundays, no phone call or emails all weekend, rarely anything meaningful on Mondays (even on those few occasions when Monday isn't a Bank Holiday. Not that I *used* to think there were too many Bank Holidays, not back when I was an employee, when Bank Holidays meant a day off for me, instead of, as now, a day off for everyone else).

Tuesday's a sort of deflated Monday. Wednesdays and Thursdays are OK, I suppose, if you like that sort of thing, but the rest is just one big weekend. Friday doesn't mean 'Plenty drinks and a curry tonight' – not to the freelance. It means 'That's the end of yet another week during which nothing good happened'.

Another thing I hate about weekends is the noise. Working at home, having the place to yourself for five days a week, you become very sensitive to the sounds of jollity and lawn-mowing made by wage slaves out on parole. Your tolerance threshold for shouts and kiddies playing and car doors slamming and radios jingling becomes dangerously low. Especially if you live in a suburb or dormitory town, you get used to owning the streets on weekdays, and you find it hard to go back to sharing them at weekends and on those endless bloody Bank Holidays.

This sense of owning the week is a pleasant one, it must be said, reminiscent of the very best days of your childhood – that is, the days when you were off school with a doctor's appointment.

Self-employed, you can go to the garden centre on a Monday instead of a Saturday. You can go into a DIY shop and find that not only have the assistants got time to answer your questions, but that they are actually grateful for your custom; grateful even for your company, grateful that you have broken the boredom of a Wednesday afternoon in November.

The only trouble is that, being self-employed, you haven't got *time* to go to the shops, on weekdays or weekends. If you are in a shop it's only because you've run out of toner for your printer. As, of course, has the shop; you can bet on that, any day of the week.

In all my years as a full-time freelance, I have never been unemployed. I have however spent many weeks and months and even one whole year *underemployed*, and at those times I have frequently earned less in a month than I would have done if I'd been on the dole.

Underemployment is one of the great horrors of freelancing. It can be very difficult to get out of, too, since the underemployed writer doesn't have time on his hands, unused hours during which he might look for new areas of work, or for another line of work altogether. Quite the opposite: the less paid work you've got on the books, the more time you have to spend working – writing on spec, contacting contacts, chasing half-promises from long ago.

One of the reasons I'm writing this book now, as opposed to a year ago or the year after next, is that I am currently underemployed – the obvious thing to do when you've got no writing work on, is to write about writing. This is known technically as 'the last stage of being desperate before total despair sets in'. It *is*, you can look it up in a medical dictionary.

I have always tried to keep my range of freelancing work as broad as possible – in terms of subjects covered, types of market and styles – in the hope that such catholicity would protect me from Suddenly Collapsing Markets Syndrome. What you do when you're underemployed is, in theory, you move sideways. If you've spent the last six months writing about football for women's magazines, and suddenly that work isn't there any more (told you going to the office party was a mistake, after you'd been using that transsexual by-line), then what you do – in theory – is start writing radio plays about rugby. Or something. You think sideways, work sideways, move sideways. This is know technically as 'a touch of the crabs'. It is.

But diversification doesn't always work, and has its own dangers. It's easy to spread yourself too thinly across the spectrum, so that you end up one atom thick and thus invisible to the editorial eye.

Besides, what tends to happen in practice is that one area of your work takes off – an editor sees you writing about aubergines, and gets you in to do some aubergine stuff for him, and then the aubergine producers' trade mag grabs you, and before long you have become Aubergine Man. Now you're doing so much aubergine-related work that you haven't any time to pursue opportunities in the kohl rabi sector. You're back where you started: when the aubergine craze dies out, you will return to the familiar embrace of under-employment.

Writers used to be able to support themselves with all sorts of mini-jobs, when times were hard: bar work, delivering leaflets, that sort of thing. But this has become much more difficult these days. Such jobs are harder to get and are even lower paid than they used to be. The reasons for this, as for everything else in human life, are economic.

What Thatcherites called 'taming the unions', and Blairites, less bluntly, call 'achieving flexible labour markets', both mean the same thing: weaker unions, less full-time male workers and more part-time female workers, and lower wages. Therefore jobs which used to provide extra income for students, housewives, the semi-retired and the self-employed are now breadwinner's jobs. There are people these days who deliver leaflets door-to-door, advertising giant indoor car boot sales, for a living.

At the same time, because wages have gone down in real jobs, so wages in mini-jobs have gone down. Writers today cannot rely as previous generations did on getting a spot of causal to tide you over when the writing isn't selling too well.

Nor can you rely, as I thought I could when I left work in the mid-80s, on returning to full-time work if freelancing doesn't work out. As soon as you pack your belongings into your carrier bag and leave the workplace for the last time, your job will have been rationalised out of existence before you get as far as the bus stop.

I'm saying, if you decide to leave work, you must assume that this decision is irreversible.

A handy checklist. Stick it to your fridge, so that you can see it every morning before going off to work.

THE TEN WORST THINGS ABOUT SELF-EMPLOYMENT

1. The money's lousy.
2. The hours stink.
3. It's all your fault.
4. No holidays.
5. No days off.
6. No sick leave.
7. No free use of facilities.
8. No one else to cunningly palm off your work on to.
9. Everything.
10. Everything else.

But if you are going to leave work, at least don't do so until you have taken the one most important preparatory step – get married. Two really can live a lot more cheaply than one, especially if one is a spouse with a decent job and the other one is a freelance writer on £5,000 a year.

Children, on the other hand, must be avoided at all costs. If you've already got some, and you're thinking of taking up freelancing, then sell the kids and buy a photocopier.

HOW TO DIE OF A BROKEN HEART

When she was a little girl, my mother had to go into hospital to have her tonsils removed. Just before the operation, the anaesthetist explained to her that she was going to be taken to a very dark room, but that she mustn't be afraid because she was going to see lots of lovely films. Mickey Mouse cartoons, to be exact.

The anaesthetist lied. Bastard. There were no cartoons. Instead, there was anaesthesia, a panicky loss of consciousness, followed by nausea and a lingering pain. Bastard.

Now, since at that time anaesthesia and kinematography both were in their infancy, you might think that my mother would have been as excited by one as by the other. But no: this was hundreds of years ago, and cartoons were a rare treat, and she was really looking forward to seeing them, and the cartoons never arrived. She had been lied to, by a professional man who had her life in his hands.

Bastard. Decades later, as she told me the story, I could still hear the bitterness in her voice. Decades later, grown up and grown out of Mickey Mouse, she was still disappointed.

Yet what can she know of disappointment, who has never worked as a freelance writer?

Disappointment is such a little, trivial, kiddie-sounding word, but I'm willing to bet that more suicides are caused by disappointment than by tragedy. (The world is shaped by strong economies and weak emotions: the role of embarrassment in human history, for instance, has never been fully documented. It is not often noted that the people who achieve things in life are generally the people who are not frightened of making fools of themselves.)

Sitting here now in my office surrounded by unpublished books and unpaid bills, I am surprised to find that I cannot remember my first great freelance disappointment. Never mind. I can remember several others, and they'll do.

Way back, when I still had a day job, I sold a piece to *The Listener*. Younger readers may have no idea what I'm talking about, but take my word for it – this was both an honour and a great step forward.

The editor's assistant rang to tell me that the editor would like to meet me. Have a drink with me. Have a chat. Next Thursday, she said. What time? I asked. Come after six, she said.

I've rarely been as excited about anything. Sipping sherry with the editor of *The Listener*! By invitation! In his office! I dressed carefully and conservatively: clean T-shirt; jeans with no sick stains; belt with professionally punched holes, not ones made with a skewer; shoes . . . well, you know, shoes.

Cleaned my teeth twice. Bought a comb, combed my hair. Had three showers: one in the morning, one when I got home from work, and another one when I got home from work. Spent the Tube journey to the West End clearing my throat, so I wouldn't have to do it when I got there. When I got there, the editor had gone home.

I forget the details now. Some mix-up, nobody's fault, I think. A difference of language, probably. In the editor's assistant's circles, 'After six' meant 'Six'; in my circles, it meant 'Half past at the very earliest, so as not to appear too uncool'. Her language was more languid than mine, but her circles were tighter.

We had our meeting eventually, the editor and I. The mix-up made no lasting difference. I wrote several more pieces for *The Listener*. But the journey home on the Tube that evening . . . I don't know how I ended it still alive, I really don't. And then ringing my girlfriend. 'You're home early. How did it go?' Oh god, it pains me to this day.

It may be that such stories do not make you cringe or weep. If so, then you are either so tough that you will, I fear, find freelancing an insufficient challenge, or else you simply have no imagination – in which case you can still be a writer, but you'll have to stick to non-genre fiction, and end up serialised on *Woman's Hour*.

Ten years after the Case of the Editor Who'd Gone, I paid £80 for a book because I was supposed to be in it. I wasn't. I was in the index, I was in the Notes on Contributors, I'd even been paid, but my piece wasn't in the book. No reason, just an error in editing.

Eighty quid! Plus postage! What made it worse what that that particular essay was one of the best things I'd ever written.

I won't go through the whole list. We haven't got the space, apart from anything else. And I'm only giving you some randomly selected lowlights here, I'm not bothering to mention the scores of times that I've sold a short story to issue five of a magazine which has gone bust after issue three, or the dozens of people who've told me for sure that the project was in the bag, and who I never heard from again, and so on and so on.

And so on. Honestly, I could fill a book.

I COULD, I COULD FILL A BOOK

Experience does help, to some extent. Some years ago, during a particularly underemployed period, I had two big possibles on the go. There was a TV series proposal I put together with an independent production company. The commissioning editor at the BBC was very keen, it was looking like a dead cert, the producer – usually the most cautiously pessimistic of men – was getting excited to the very verge of hubris about our prospects. And then the BBC rearranged its commissioning procedures, and our proposal fell through the cracks, dead as a pickled herring.

Meanwhile, I'd had a phone call from a radio producer I'd done some work with. Her boss wanted me to send in a CV, and samples of my writing. The boss was crazy about me, loved my work, something big and exciting was about to happen. Naturally, I never heard any more.

I wasn't disappointed. I've trained myself not to believe in big exciting things, and after a while, the training becomes second nature. Most of the time.

If you make sure you never get excited, you'll never get disappointed. At the same time, of course, if you make sure you never get disappointed, you're never going to have any excitement.

I warn you most earnestly: if you think you might be the sort of person who might be killed by disappointment, you must find another way of making a living, some other way of making a life. Haemophiliacs should not work in pin factories and people who are vulnerable to destruction by disappointment should not work in writing.

I'm not exaggerating: as a freelance, disappointment will be your constant shadow. You will get more disappointments than you get hot meals, sex and birthday cards put together. It will be a very rare month indeed that doesn't involve at least one crushing disappointment. Get three or four of those in one fortnight, and it really does take a certain strength of will to carry on working. Or just to carry on breathing.

There is nothing you can do about it, except to prepare yourself mentally as far as possible. Train yourself to know and to believe that nothing is ever going to turn out right.

Never believe anything until it's actually happened, and you've actually got paid for it. If you can manage not to believe it even when it has happened and you have been paid for it, then as far as I'm concerned you are not psychotic, you are merely employing all reasonable caution. You are ahead of the game.

You will never get paid on time.

I'll say it again: you will *never* get paid on time. It's going to be for the best if you can understand this – really understand it, and accept it – right from the start. With that knowledge in your heart, you might be able to lessen some of the anger and frustration that awaits you, if you're ever lucky enough to sell anything.

Before writing this piece, I spent a little time trying to work out whether something that I often tell people is actually true: namely, that I spend more time chasing cheques than I do writing. And then I realised that this working-out was not only behaviour verging on the obsessive, but that it was also a terrible waste of time which would be better spent chasing cheques. So I stopped.

I don't know a freelance who doesn't spend part of just about every week working on debt collection. I probably don't know a self-employed person of any sort who is accustomed to getting paid on time. I can only think of one or two employers, in the entire universe of freelance writing, who can be relied upon to pay up when they say they'll pay up.

I remember the rich entertainer who owed me one thousand pounds for months and months. A grand is a lot of money to me, a hell of a lot of money, but to a rich entertainer a grand is the pizza budget for a lively weekend. And there's your problem, mate, right there: how can a man to whom a thousand pounds is nothing possibly understand why the man he owes the thousand pounds to is making such an almighty fuss about it?

I beat the rich entertainer about the ear with violent language. I threatened him with legal action. Eventually, I forced myself to calm down and think the thing through, and that was when I came up with the answer: I told the rich entertainer that if he didn't pay me by the end of the week, I'd never talk to him again. That did the trick; two things that are worth knowing about entertainers are that none of them ever laugh off duty, and that all of them are terrified that nobody really likes them. A third thing worth knowing is that they tend to be almost clinically tight with cash, though often generous with booze, drugs, affection and hospitality.

Even then, I had to walk the rich entertainer round to his building society, and physically take the banker's cheque from his reluctant hand.

A grand is, at least, a sum worth chasing. But I have wasted uncountable hours of my short-and-brutal in pursuit of much smaller sums.

There used to be a free magazine in London which refused to pay its contributors their agreed fees as a matter of policy. The publisher knew that freelances couldn't afford to sue, so, he obviously figured, why bother even pretending to pay them? The most amazing aspect of this story is that there were freelances who wrote for him *more than once*. That must be pretty close to a dictionary definition of desperate. Pretty damn close to a dictionary definition of freelancing, too.

Years ago, when I was just starting out, I wrote a piece about pubs for this same magazine, for an agreed fee of thirty pounds, which of course never appeared. Logically, I should have just let it go after the first few weeks of frustration; but logic is a poor salve to a cheated man. The amount of money I spent in vain pursuit of my thirty quid is a sum I would rather not work out. I wasted time, I wasted postage, and I wasted half a quarterly phone bill, ringing them, at one stage, every hour on the hour for four days solid. I hope my campaign of telephonic terrorism annoyed the magazine's staff, but it didn't get me paid.

(The mag subsequently went out of business. Part of the reason, I like to think, is that for the next two years I went out every week, found as many of the free mag's unmanned PLEASE TAKE ONE bins as I could, and tore every single copy in half.)

Big organisations can be better than small ones, or than individuals, at paying up, because they have a bureaucracy dedicated to accounting. On the other hand, I'm writing this particular chapter on this particular day mainly because I have spent most of this week trying to get the BBC to cough up a hundred quid repeat fee, which is two months overdue. (It's been quite a week all round, in fact. In the same post that didn't contain the BBC cheque I received one from a newspaper which was £100 short, and I'm still waiting for an income tax rebate of several hundred quid. Tax rebates don't come automatically, let alone swiftly, but have to be applied for in writing, despite the fact that it is *my* bleeding money, which I generously leant the government, which probably spent it on Trident submarines, when I paid tax on last year's better figures. All together, I'm short of over one thousand pounds, all of which is mine, all of which I should have had ages ago, and all of which I have already spent – on fripperies like the phone bill and having the central heating serviced.)

Of course, the BBC doesn't deliberately withhold payment – but the very bureaucracy which ensures eventual settlement frequently produces human errors and computer farts which can delay cheques for weeks or months.

Big, respectable institutions do rip writers off, but usually by accident. The very first thing I ever sold the BBC was a sketch about a vicar, for a radio comedy show called *The [David] Jason Explanation*. My friend Gary and I wrote reams of material on spec, and were sufficiently hardened to the ways of light ent not to be too devastated when we didn't hear anything back. But I listened to the series even so, and was numb with thrillfulness when I heard one of our bits, a quite neat pull-back-to-reveal quickie, on the episode entitled *The Jason Explanation of Saturday Night*.

I waited, excitedly, for the closing credits, to hear for the first time my name listed as a contributor to a comedy show (what? Oh yeah, and Gary's name too, yeah, obviously). And it didn't happen: we weren't in the credits.

I spent ages looking for a phone box that worked so that I could tell Gary about our major career breakthrough – that of being treated like shit, the way real writers are, for the first time – before remembering that Gary wasn't on the phone, and . . . Anyway, the producer (who went on to be quite a big name as a comedy writer/performer/producer/impresario) had probably stuck our sketch in at the last minute, to make up the running time, and forgotten to amend the paperwork (the opposite happened to me a few years later, when I was credited on screen at the end of a *Spitting Image* election special, though my contribution had been cut before transmission).

Took us a while to get the cheque for the *Jason* sketch, but we did get it in the end. Gary suggested we keep it as a souvenir, I suggested we spend it on Guinness, so in the end we compromised, and spent it on Guinness. That series has been repeated a few times, and on each occasion we've received another little cheque, no prob.

But you know what I think'd be nice? I think it'd be nice if, next time the BBC puts out *The Jason Explanation of Saturday Night*, the broadcast ends with solemn martial music and an announcer says, in a very deep voice, 'The Corporation wishes to acknowledge the enormous immense contribution made by Mat and Gary's epoch-making Vicar Quickie to the programme you have just heard, and indeed to the subsequent success of Mr David Jason's entire career'. I don't suppose Gary would be that bothered – he's a teacher now, with a pension to look forward to, sensible man – but I think it would be an appropriate gesture.

IT GETS WORSE Even if you do get your cheque on time, you should be aware that 'on time' doesn't mean here what it does in most other commercial relationships. When you buy a packet of fags from an off licence, you pay for it there and then. When you sell an article to a nationally distributed magazine, you will, if you're lucky, get paid a month after publication.

Before I became a full-time freelance, I used to work for the London Borough of Camden. Here is an example of the kind of conversation that I never ever had with the wages section at Camden Town Hall:

> **ME**: Hello, I wonder if you can help me. Thing is, see, I haven't been paid for two months, and I'm starving to death, and the landlord's getting nasty, and I was just wondering –
>
> **WAGES CLERK**: Yeah, right, you and half of London, man, if that's any comfort! No, seriously, sorry about that, but what's actually happening, right, let me tell you the situation, see, what it is, the guy who's supposed to be doing the cheques, right, he's off sick, yeah, his dad got run over and killed by a hearse, shouldn't laugh really, it's a real mess, like. And *unfortu-nate-lee*, yeah, I know it sounds daft, right, but the problem is that nobody else here has actually got this guy's actual, like, codes and that. Yeah? You with me? So basically, it's like a bit of a

mess and that, and the thing is, right, as luck would have it, this guy's got like two weeks leave due starting next week, right? But listen, I'll tell you what, if you could just *bear with me* for, like, another two or three weeks, then as soon as he gets back, like, I'll put a note on his desk, and *with a bit of luck*, like, he should be able to sort you out in time for Christmas. OK, yeah? Tell you the truth, mate, it is a bit of a bloomin' mad house here right now, to be honest, it's like, y'know – you don't have to be mad to work here, but if you are you get extra luncheon vouchers, you know what I mean?

Book contracts usually provide for the payment of the author's advance in three parts: a third on signature, a third on delivery, a third on publication. Sounds fair. But in practice, you may very well still be waiting for part two – and quite possibly part one – after your book has come out, failed to sell, disappeared, and been pulped.

There was one basically honest magazine publisher that didn't manage to pay me for about six months because they kept losing my address. They were very nice about it, and everything, but all the same . . .

So, I live on my credit cards (having spent my wits years ago). And it's lucky I applied for those cards when I was still an employee, because you've got sod all chance of getting so much as a cheque book out of a bank these days without producing six months' worth of pay slips and a reference from your boss.

I waste my time, I get into debt, I daily risk death from apoplexy . . . and that is during the good times. That's when I'm working. I can gauge how well my business is going not by how much tax I pay, but by how many hours of each week I spend chasing cheques.

You will never get paid on time.

Not only won't you get paid on time, but you will rarely be paid the right amount. *Au contraire*, you will probably be paid the wrong amount repeatedly. A while ago, I did a series of small jobs for a national newspaper. For each piece I was underpaid by fifty quid on the agreed fee. The editor assured me each time that the missing money would be added, accumulatively, to the next cheque. But each time . . . you get the picture.

And if a magazine is struggling, or about to go bust, then freelance contributors are the last people to get paid because everyone knows they won't do anything about it, they'll just keep writing, because – what else is there to do?

If this bothers you – I mean, if this bothers you so much that you know you couldn't live with it; if this bothers you so much that you simply don't believe it, you think I must be exaggerating – then here's what you do. You get a day job with a firm which pays weekly or monthly wages into your bank account by direct credit. Yes, I know that system can go wrong too, but at least it won't go wrong *every single time*.

Some obvious questions thus arise:

1. When should I start chasing my money?

My advice is to start chasing it before it's due. If the job is for a big organisation, then the person commissioning you won't be the person who actually pays the money. This can make the process easier, since your contact is less likely to take it personally when you start agitating for your overdue fee. However, be prepared for it to *become* personal, if necessary. Don't be fooled into talking to the accounts department; they do nothing all day but talk to disgruntled contributors, and will not be impressed by your pleading, cursing and threats of suicide. Instead, ensure that every contact you make is through the editorial staff – disrupt their lives sufficiently, and they might be sufficiently motivated to expedite your payment.

Start, though, by saying, at the time that you agree the details of the job, 'Incidentally, mate, any chance of rushing that cheque through a bit? Only I've just had this fat bastard of a phone bill, and quite frankly things are looking a touch dodgy'. Your editor isn't going to take pity on you and go into battle on your behalf against the accounts department, but you have at least put him on notice that you're not going to be patient when the cheque doesn't arrive.

In a smaller set-up, the person you're speaking to probably *is* the person who's paying you, and that can make things more embarrassing, and more dangerous in terms of preserving the writer-editor relationship. My advice is still to start chasing as early as possible, but you could try disguising the chase as one element in a wide-ranging conversation:

'Hi, man, how's it hanging? Yeah, yeah, great . . . So, how's the gonorrhoea, any better? Huh? Oh, sorry, it's just you were telling us all about it at that office party the other week, and I didn't know it was supposed to be a . . . Yeah, of course, rely on me. Mum's the word. Anyway, hey, I'm going to be down your way next week, thought we might snatch a drop of lunch, yeah? Great. Save you a stamp as well, if you happen to have my cheque ready by then . . .'

Don't be too subtle though. You're dealing with editors, remember.

2. How should I chase?

As long as you want to remain on speaking terms with the employer in question, and as long as you want to have a chance of eventually getting the dosh, the answer has to be 'politely and persistently'. If you've ever seen an unusually well trained beat cop persuading a respectable drunk to move along, you'll know what I mean: 'If you could see your way to pulling up your trousers and taking that briefcase off your head, sir, that'd be much appreciated . . . There you go, smashing, good chap.'

3. When should I give up chasing?

Ha! Well, if you are so confident of your sanity that you believe you will ever be *able* to give up – then I would say, once you have burned down their offices, killed their children, and killed their children's children: *that's* a good time to give up.

A BRIEF HISTORY OF INFLATION

According to an *Observer* review of *Later Short Stories* by Anthony Trollope, these stories are ones which 'Trollope deftly knocked off at six guineas a page right up to his death in 1882'.

Six guineas a page! Can you imagine what a fortune that must have been in 1882? I have sold stories to professional, prestigious outlets in the *2000s* which have paid considerably less than six pounds thirty pence per page. So not only has the rate at which freelance writers are paid fallen during this century, dramatically, in adjusted terms, which we all knew; it has also, we now discover, fallen in pound-for-pound terms.

Depressing, isn't it?

Not that there's such a thing as a rate for the job – or rather, there are rates, negotiated between the unions and the employers' organisations, for big jobs, like writing an episode of *The Bill*, but most of your work is likely to be found in the netherworld of dribs'n'drabs, where the rate for the job is what you can get.

Writers moan about the money they make, but really that's just part of the job description; writers are required under the terms of their code of conduct to moan about fees, just as farmers are obliged to moan about the weather. The truth is, the money you can get just for a bit of ol' scribbling is bloody fantastic. In fact, freelance writing is a tremendously well-paid occupation.

I am nowhere near the high-class end of the trade, and yet I am often given two hundred quid for a job that's going to take me a couple of days at most. I know people who work forty hours a week in factories and take home less than that.

However: those factory workers are taking home that money every week. It's guaranteed, this week, next week, every week – at least until their factory gets crated up and shipped off to South Korea in order to 'make our economy more competitive'.

My two hundred pounds might be – there's no real reason to suppose it won't be – the last I ever earn. Besides which, there are all the days to be taken into the calculation when nobody was paying me; days spent chasing work, or doing my accounts, or catching up with reading stuff that, maybe, some time later, might enable me to take on a job that will earn me £200.

Freelance writing is like real life in this one respect: that the effort and skill which go into a job bear no relation to how much you get paid for it. Just as the chairman of the National Lottery gets paid ten thousand times as much as a traffic warden, despite his work being ten million times less demanding, less effortful, and less useful to society, so I've done jobs which took weeks, required specialist skills and hard labour, and paid almost nothing per hour, and other jobs which involved little more than saying 'Good Morning' in a funny voice, and for which I received a fortnight's wages.

One of my regular gigs in particular pays so little that I'd probably be better off getting a little man in to do it for me, and deducting him against tax. I took it on ages ago, during a period when I was desperate for work. In good times, this chore is extremely un-cost effective, as it is one which uses up a lot of hours for little return. I've often been tempted to dump it, but the memory of how glad I was to have it when I first accepted it, and how often I have been glad of it during lean times since, makes me pause.

Never make the mistake of thinking you've made it. Never start behaving as if you've made it – like, for instance, dumping time-gobbling, low-paid jobs that have been useful to you in the past – without being absolutely sure that you're never going to need them again.

In freelancing, you've never made it. This year you could earn £25,000 – next year £2,500. Happens all the time. Believe me.

MONEY FOR NOTHING

You'll read a lot about 'kill fees' in the type of HowToWrite that's written by someone who's never written anything. The professional freelance, they tell you, always agrees a fee up front, and at the same time agrees a kill fee – that is, a proportion of the agreed fee which will be paid if, for some reason, the piece isn't used after all.

I'd be lying if I said I'd never received a kill fee, but I could probably count the number of such payments on the fingers of one hand. Even if the hand belonged to Captain Hook.

Very early on I received a kill fee from *The Listener*, for a commissioned piece which the editor didn't like at all, but that was only because that particular editor was a good bloke who liked to encourage young writers. (I then sold the article to *Midweek* magazine, my first ever submission to them, so I was well pleased.)

But I certainly didn't agree the kill fee in advance. Can you imagine doing that? 'OK, we've agreed the payment, now look, just supposing the piece I eventually turn in is such a staggeringly misformed pig's breakfast that you can't possibly run it without permanently damaging your reputation – how much you gonna pay me then, huh?' This approach would not, I suggest, do a lot to build up your 'professional' standing.

Of course there will be times when it isn't your fault at all that a piece of work isn't used;

a change of management, for instance, or an editorial page lost to a last-minute advert. And under those circumstances you're undoubtedly entitled to your money – *all* your money, never mind a poxy kill fee. Whether you'll get it depends, I suppose, on the kind of editor you're working for, the kind of organisation he is employed by, and the kind of relationship you have with him, and what value he attaches to that relationship. And, sometimes, how far you are willing to push it.

Be assertive in pursuit of your rights by all means, but also remember that a kill fee in the hand isn't worth a dozen potential future commissions ending up in someone else's bush. Sorta thing.

HOW TO GO MAD

I didn't do any work at all yesterday. I spent the whole day on the phone to the bank, trying to find what had happened to a small cheque which they had lost – although 'lost' isn't a word they care for. They insist that, since the cheque has been cleared, but has not appeared in my account, it must have been stolen. Stolen, eh? By a gang of international jewel thieves fallen on hard times, presumably.

What's really happened is that the bank has paid the cheque into the wrong account. But you could threaten them with firebombing, and you still wouldn't get the bastards to admit responsibility. (Late postscript: I eventually persuaded the bank to pay me ten pounds compensation. When it didn't arrive I chased them for it, sending them the same fax ten times in one day at half hour intervals. Three days later, they faxed me back to apologise again, and to say that they would now be paying fifteen quid into my account as compensation for their mistake concerning compensation for their mistake. The last line of the fax pretty much sums up the impossibility of getting any sense out of any modern, computerised corporation: 'I enclose a copy of the Working Together Leaflet as requested'. Not only had I not requested any such thing – but how do you 'enclose' a leaflet with a fax message?)

By the end of my day spent banker-bothering, I was shaking with rage and frustration, almost exploding with anger and impotence. Of course, this is not a problem unique to writers, or to the self-employed. These days – with computerisation, deregulation, mergers, and American-style management training programmes – it is very rare for a bank, or any similar organisation, to get anything right, ever. You all know this. You've all wasted hours of your short lives struggling with a bureaucracy which is either crooked or incompetent, or usually both.

But here's the difference. As a self-employed person, I am entirely at the mercy of large organisations against which I have no redress whatsoever. There are people living on the streets of all our cities right now, begging for a living, waiting to die, who used to have homes and jobs and marriages – until their bank paid a cheque into the wrong account. Literally.

A few years ago I made the awful mistake of buying a computer by mail order from a firm called MJN. It didn't work. I spent several weeks trying to get MJN to do something about that, until I eventually gave up and paid a local computer geezer to come round and fix the fucking thing at my expense. He was here for an hour (a component in the thingy had been plugged into the wrong bit of the whatsit) and he charged me £25. I was happy.

Well, happy and wishing I was dead at the same time, if you know what I mean. I had lost time and income. I had spent an incalculable amount of money on phone and fax, desperately trying to get MJN to put their mistake right, or at least to give me some helpful advice, or even to answer the phone, let alone call me back when they said they would. This is the short version I'm giving you, you understand. I've left out my thoughts on the amazing ignorance of the dull-witted telesales clerks who staff what computer companies have the stunning cheek to call 'technical support lines'.

That MJN business came at a bad time. A couple of months earlier I had gone through weeks of same-as-above with British Telecom, the well-known privatised anti-utility, the notorious mafia-run gang of Satanist baby-stranglers. Yeah, you must have heard of them.

I'd moved house, and I needed two phone lines, for my phone and fax. BT took more than a month to perform that complicated task. Though, naturally, they didn't tell me at the beginning it was going to take them that long. And did you know that BT's complaints department and/or head office aren't listed, either in BT's telephone directory or with BT's directory enquiries? In fact, when you ring BT the person you speak to will tell you that 'There is no complaints department, and we don't have a head office, as such'.

At least BT eventually paid me a very small amount of compensation (nothing for lost income though – that isn't policy). And after I had written a magazine column about all this, naming names, I even received a letter of apology from the (allegedly non-existent) chairman's office. Or, anyway, from someone who works in an office which is on the same floor as the chairman's office.

I won't go on, though I could. I'll just point out again, because you really do want to think about this before you take any irrevocable career decisions, that for an employed person, this kind of adventure in corporate hell are very irritating and very expensive, in wasted time and money. But that if you're self-employed, they can be fatal: to you, or even worse, to your business.

An editor rings you to offer you a commission. He can't get through, because your phone's buggered. OK, suppose he's an exceptionally patient editor (*yeah* . . .), so he writes to you. You still can't accept his offer, because your computer doesn't work. Or because, if you don't spend the next six days on the phone to your bank, they are going to declare you terminally overdrawn, cancel your cheque book, refuse your standing orders, and charge you a hundred quid in made-up-on-the-spot fees (they charge you for sorting out their own mistakes nowadays, did you know *that*?).

When you're a full-time freelance writer you soon learn that the phrase hand-to-mouth isn't just another empty cliché; you come to understand exactly what it means. It is resonant, starkly descriptive, brutally accurate. It is you. It is your life, your days and weeks, your future. You can go bust in less time than it takes for the Abbey-sodding-National to answer the phone. If your phone happens to be working that week, I mean.

I know at least two formerly self-employed people who are now living, just about, on state benefits because of mistakes they didn't make. The only mistake they made was in imagining that large companies operate honestly, or give a damn whether their customers live or die.

And there's nothing you can do about it. Not until I get round to finishing my next book, *How to Take Revenge on Large Companies in a Manner Which Involves the Infliction of Actual Physical Damage Through Three Generations of Devilspawn*, anyway.

You can buy your computer from a local dealer, you can bank with the Co-op (who do make mistakes, but at least they don't make a profit; the Co-op Bank is owned by its customers), you can keep a mobile phone for emergencies. But understand: you can be a good writer, working hard, working well, doing everything you should be doing, and you can still be destroyed, between now and Christmas, if a couple of computer operators nod off for a few seconds in an office complex somewhere on Merseyside.

So just tell me this: why the hell do you want to leave work? Do you have no idea at all when you're well off?

All right, there is something you can do. It's not much and it doesn't always work and it involves you spending even more time and money and you'll have to think carefully about whether or not it's worth it. And if you're not careful, it can be dangerous. But yes, there is something you can do.

I call it frothing.

Recently, I frothed another bank into giving me ten quid compensation. They'd made their third computer error in a week on my account (which I have since closed). This resulted in them sending me a dunning letter.

I was pretty angry, as you can imagine; none of us are at out calmest in the mornings, are we? Perhaps there should be a law, no postal deliveries before 1pm. So I decided – or my synapses decided, who knows which – that it was time for a frothing.

I'm a bit of a method actor when it comes to the old froth, so before dialling the bank's Customer Couldn't-Care-Less Line I stomped around my office for a while, growling, spitting, howling, like you imagine Oliver Reed did before they slapped on the hairy make-up in that werewolf film.

Soon, I had tears in my eyes, and a sore throat, and a rapid, irregular heartbeat. I was all jazzed up and electric. If you'd seen me just then you'd have wet yourself, honest you would.

MAKING MADNESS YOUR ONLY FRIEND

If not from fear, then from laughing.

Now I dialled. As soon as the phone was answered, not even waiting to hear if it was Mandi or Juli who sought to serve me today, I jumped in. *'Soup visor! Soup visor! Gimme soup visor Now Now Now!'* My voice is higher than normal, slightly distorted, shaky. It's a voice on the edge of cracking, a voice that has you reaching for the alarm button. The voice of a soul in torment. A voice that froths at the mouth. A voice that blags compensation payments from bastard banks.

There are rules of course, of course there are rules for frothing. You'll have to make your own, but you can use these as a guide.

1. Don't go in too hard at the person who answers the phone. Remember, she is a victim of the company the same as you are. Always demand to speak to a supervisor, and preferably to a supervisor's supervisor (one of the advantages of frothing is that it gets you through the hierarchy quicker than any amount of polite pleading and reasoning). Go as high up the company ladder as you can; anyone who accepts promotion from the basic level, we must assume for the purposes of this war, knows what they're doing and gets what they deserve.

2. Remember that most large corporations now routinely tape their phone calls, for reasons of security and in case of legal action against them by their shafted customers. So write a script before you dial, and stick to it. Don't be aggressive or threatening – that justifies them in considering themselves the victim and you the victimiser, and acting accordingly. Instead, come over all suicidal and bonkers. That way, they will definitely feel uncomfortable, and may even feel guilty. Either way, they will be eager to end their contact with you as soon as possible – which means on your terms.

3. Break down sobbing every now and then, and say things like 'I'm self-employed, yeah? This bloody bank's gonna kill me, I mean *literally* it is going to kill me! I mean, what the hell's the point of carrying on when the bank just seems to be doing everything it can to close down my business!' You're walking a fine line here, though: if you get them too rattled there's a danger of them keeping you talking while they send the cops round to stop you topping yourself. That could be embarrassing.

4. If you think it's necessary and appropriate, throw in a few meaningless, tormented burbles: 'It's not there is a camel drop the rice, is it? Eh? Eh? Are you listening to me, I say it's not there is a camel drop the rice is it? IS IT?'

It's all a bit distasteful, really, the whole business of frothing. I tend to keep it for absolute emergencies, and even then I can't pretend it doesn't leave a nasty tang in the mouth. But it's a tough business being self-employed, and, hey, ten quid is ten quid.

HOW TO STOP WRITING

This appeared at the end of an otherwise straightforward piece of market info in a writers' mag: 'And remember, if you are a pessimist you will never succeed as a writer. Determination and perseverance win out in the end'.

Bollocks! We're always being told – not just as writers, but at school, at work, everywhere that the system lies to people – that if you're good enough and you work hard enough sooner or later you'll make it. This dishonest and cruel maxim lies indeed at the very heart of the dishonest and cruel HowToWrite industry.

The truth, easily divined by a moment's serious thought, is that alternative history is littered with people who never got anywhere because they weren't in the right place at the right time; people like Shakespeare, or Galton and Simpson.

The conventional advice is keep going, never give up, try try try again, both generally and with specific projects. This is clearly correct, as almost any writer could tell you from his own experiences – although my list of projects which have never got anywhere no matter how often I've tried, tried and tried again, continues to grow, and includes the groundbreaking *Bumper Book of Not Terribly Funny Jokes*, and my pet pop project, an album called *Famous People Who Can't Sing Sing The Velvet Underground*.

Your own mind is your worst enemy, obviously, when it comes to keeping going or giving up. Working on this book today, I happened to chance on a bit of it which I'd written two months earlier. It was hilarious! God, but I was a good writer in those days! If I could only somehow regain the freshness, the spontaneity, the original wit I had back then! This happens to me every time I read something I wrote more than about a week ago.

(It goes without saying, so I'll thank you for not saying it, that *you* can't tell the difference between the bits I wrote when I was brilliant and the bits I'm writing now that I'm crap.)

However, the implication that the 'keep going' advice contains is that if you keep going you will succeed, as if the universe were run along Boy Scout lines, rewarding effort and perseverance irrespective of talent or merit, and rewarding talent and merit according to desert.

This model of the universe, popular amongst pre-Marxian philosophers, is obviously flawed, as even the most cursory materialistic examination of objective reality will quickly reveal. The fact is that of all the would-be writers who never give up, who keep going, who work hard, who plug away at it cheerfully year after year, *almost none* of them will ever make it even as far as the starting line.

In other words, if you do give up, if you don't keep going, then failure is guaranteed. And if you keep going, and don't give up, then failure is almost guaranteed.

Everybody says you've got to believe in yourself, but I disagree. I think too many people believe in themselves with too little cause. Rather, you've got to know whether or not you *should* believe in yourself. Although having said that (got time for another paradox, Doctor? Just a small one), any reasonable person who was honest with themselves when starting out as a freelance would say they didn't have a chance of making it. In which case they'd give up, and no one would ever become a writer. Hmm.

This is what you should do. Analyse yourself as honestly as you can, and if you do seem to be one of those people who just believes in yourself because believing in yourself is a good thing in an idealistic, non-materialistic, non-empirical, semi-trance-state, women's-magazine kind of way, then forget it. I guarantee you have no talent, or even any of the qualities that it takes to be a successful freelance. The more you believe in yourself in this vacuous way, it seems to me, the less likely you are ever to make anything of yourself.

Lots of people start off their adult lives hoping or meaning or vaguely planning to become writers, and there's nothing particularly worrying, from a medical point of view, about that. It's a common enough phenomenon of late adolescence, along with sexual experimentation, extreme tastes in clothing and music, and a tendency towards homicidal gang-related violence.

What you must try and avoid, however, is ending up as one of those really very pitiable people who spend their whole lives *going back* to vaguely planning to become writers. Every few months, every few years, they start another book, another nightschool class, another Hypnotise Yourself To Genius correspondence course, and with each failed attempt it becomes increasingly obvious to everyone who knows them, and probably to themselves, that they are never going to do it. This can only cause unhappiness and self-contempt. And, indeed, general contempt.

I'm not referring here to people who've yet to get round to writing – as we all know, some successful writers don't get going until they're in their forties or their sixties. Nor do I mean people who've written and written for years and who haven't yet had any significant success; if they think it's worth carrying on, well, who knows, their breakthrough might come at any moment. It won't, obviously, but it *might*.

The people I'm talking about here are the ones who, for as long as you've known them, in their teens, in their twenties, in their thirties, in the kitchen at their children's fifth birthday parties, have always talked about how they're going to start writing *seriously*, starting from next Tuesday, whereas what they actually do is they actually sit around their whole lives watching TV or enrolling on college courses. Twenty years after you first met them, they're still at it. 'I've got this great idea for a sitcom, if only I could just get down to, you know, writing it . . .'

Clearly, these non-writers are a particular sub-genre of would-be writers. Like most wouldys, they lack the discipline, the drive, the determination – the desire, most probably

– to actually write. What differentiates them from other types who want to write but haven't got what it takes, is that for these ones not-writing is a lifelong curse. They are trapped in this hopeless cycle of self-disgust and disappointment; trapped by their inability to stop trying to become writers. They are addicts. They need help.

Or strangling.

People who don't know how or when to give up wishing they were writers measure everything else in their lives against their failure to achieve writerhood. Whatever else they do, whatever other successes they may accomplish, they still walk around staring at the ground, they still consider themselves failures, just because they haven't finished the novel they began when they were seventeen. Haven't finished it in the sense that they haven't yet quite got round to thinking of a title or a plot or a theme or a lead character or a setting. Haven't finished it in the sense of haven't begun it.

It is possible to escape. I've known several people who always meant to write and who did, finally, do it: they sold one novel, one radio play, or one whatever, and then they were able to stop. That was it, they'd done it, the ghost was laid. Their adolescence was at an end, and they could begin their adult lives at last.

For others it's not so easy.

The important thing of course as with all such problems is to recognise that you've got a problem.

Say 'I am not a writer'.

Empower yourself to say 'I never will be a writer'.

Work to liberate the freedom from writing which lives within your inner child's spiritual and psychic highway network of love and permissioning self-worth. Type of thing.

Surrender control of your life to a higher power which enables you to say 'I have not written today. I shall not write tomorrow. I am me and I love and respect me for who I am, a Non-Writing Individual. I do not need to write to have my own dignity in life. I have joined the pub quiz team instead'.

Or, you can find out whether or not you're suited to the freelancing life with our unique teatime quiz!

1. Do you believe that regular wages, sick pay, employment rights and security in old age are a load of girlie stuff for pansies?

    a: *Yes.*

    b: *No.*

    c: *I don't understand the question. Is it supposed to be funny or something?*

2. Do you have or have you ever had a mentor or series of mentors? Is there someone – doesn't have to be the proprietor of the *New Yorker*, could be a small press editor – who thinks your stuff is good, who champions your cause, who is as puzzled as you are that you aren't famous yet, even if you've only earned ten pounds from writing in the last ten years? If not, do you suppose this is because:

    a: *They're all ganging up on you because they don't like the way you look.*

    b: *No. (NB: 'No' is not a valid response to this particular question.)*

    c: *What sort of quiz is this? Where are the questions about 'Who usually initiates lovemaking, you or your partner?'*

3. From what distance can you tell whether or not your post contains an unforeseen cheque, or an exciting acceptance, or an unexpected commission, or news of a thrilling new market, or just the usual pile of old mandelson?

    a: *I can tell by looking at the post as the postie sorts it out while walking up my drive. In fact, I can tell by looking at the postie's face as he sits in his van finishing his fag, halfway down the next street.*

    b: *That's nothing, that is. I can tell even before I open the door of my flat, I can tell as my silent neighbour riffles through the post in the communal hall, I can tell by the sound by the smell by the taste of the mail on the breeze of the morn. I can tell you exactly what my post contains long before it is even posted. The knowledge burns inside me, deep inside me, like a sacred flame. It burns, it burns. It burns, it burns.*

    c: *This is just silly, isn't it? I mean, how can you tell what post you've got until you've got it? Hey? You see, all that is that is just silliness, that's all that is.*

4. Do you think it is ever possible under any circumstances for change of any kind not to be bad news for a freelance writer?

a: Yes, as it happens, I do, though I can't think of any examples off the top of my head.

b: From the way this question is phrased I deduce that the required answer is No. Therefore my answer is No.

c: I'm not playing. This is childish.

How Did You Score?

Mostly A's: What are you doing now? You are actually *looking up* the answers? Bloody hell! Have you any idea just precisely how pathetic that is? Go away!

A BRIEF WORD ON THE WORD STUFF

The stuff that you write is, throughout the writing business, known almost invariably as 'stuff'. Years ago, the poetry editor of a weekly magazine sent me a note to tell me that she 'really liked my stuff'. And the funny thing is, she really did: she used quite a lot of it.

Ever since then I have always thought of everything I write as *stuff*: at first ironically, but in the end automatically. Stuff.

Which is why the word stuff appears so often in this book. If you want to sound like an insider, if you yearn for authentic writer's jargon with which to adorn your persona, then there you are: stuff. Pronounced as spelt.

There: now you're one of us.

AFTER TAKING LUNCH WITH MOTORHEAD, THE
EDITOR OF SMASH SOUNDS LOOKS KEENLY
AT YOUR MANUSCRIPT...

2: Save time, fail from the start

My first big sale? Yes, of course I remember my first big sale. But first let me tell you about my first sale.

Like most stories, it starts before it starts, and we haven't got room for all that, so I'll start it here:

I came out of a phone box – a proper old red pre-Regime phone box, one that smelt of piss and baccy – into the petrol and leaf smell of a sunny autumn day in Hampstead. As I emerged from that phone box I had no job, no money, no plans and I was recovering from a nasty stomach bug. I was Superman's negative.

So I did what you'd have done; I went into the nearest second-hand bookshop (I should perhaps explain that in those days the pubs shut for several hours in the afternoon).

This was the bookshop in Flask Walk which some of you will know; an old, twisty building full of stacks and shelves and ancient wood and poor light – a fine place. I went straight to the humour section, to see if they'd got in any Ronald Searle books since I'd last looked, and they hadn't, but they had got a jacketless 1938 hardback called *Darts With The Lid Off* by Alan and Geoffrey D'Egville, which I bought for 50p. I have been a mad keen darts fan since my teens, and was at that time a mad keen dart player, too; in fact, I had an important league match that night (in which I won both my games, just for the record).

Darts With The Lid Off is a sort of *1066 and all that* history of darts, and what struck me about it was that, while very much of its period, most of its jokes and observations worked just as well, and were just as relevant, fifty years later.

Using that as my (admittedly unoriginal) angle, I wrote an article about this forgotten book for *Darts World* magazine. It sold immediately – for £25, I think.

Strictly, this wasn't my first ever professional sale, but it was the first one that led somewhere; and things leading somewhere is, to a large extent, what freelancing is all about. For a while I wrote a monthly humour column for *Darts World*, 'The A–Z of Darts'. That fizzled out after a few months, the way things do – things fizzling out on you is to a large extent what freelancing is all about – but it was my first regular column, my first commission, and I am as pleased about it today as I was then.

It's a trick I've tried several times since: finding some quaint gem in a second hand bookshop, and then writing a clearly targeted piece about it. But for some reason, it's never worked again. I've found the books, I've written the articles, but I have never again succeeded in placing one.

Which is a pity, because it's a perfectly sound idea, a sensible, well-thought out strategy, and the fact that it doesn't often work just goes to show that – well, that sensible strategies and good ideas and justice aren't necessarily what freelancing is all about.

The newspaper humorist Beachcomber had a gag that went something like 'SEVEN HORSES WEDGED UP A CHIMNEY: The story to fit this headline has not yet turned up'. Apart from being one of the best funny lines ever written, that's also not a bad guide to how to have ideas.

For humour writers, having ideas isn't, or shouldn't be, all that difficult. It's largely a matter of turning things on their heads, looking at commonplace situations or linguistic constructs mirrorwise, and of making a written note of any small thing which strikes you as funny, odd, or in any way noteworthy.

A few years ago, when I was writing a weekly bits and pieces column for a general interest magazine, I got a lot of mileage out of the way my primitive wordprocessor's spellchecker turned people's names into words. The machine's suggested alternatives were often amusingly appropriate, and so every week for a while I would run a themed batch of names – politicians, sportsmen, TV personalities – through the spellcheck, and then turn the list produced into a narrative paragraph.

The idea (the thing that transformed a serendipitous one-joke phenomenon into something that I could earn from) was that my spellchecker was a kind of fortune-telling machine, which revealed hidden truths about the celebrities it renamed.

A columnist on another paper managed to fill some of his space even more easily – by reprinting some of my best examples. This wasn't stealing, since he began his piece with the magic words 'I am indebted to Mat Coward of *Midweek* magazine for the following'. As I happen to know that he was being paid a great deal more for his column than I was being paid for mine, his borrowing of my idea is a very fine demonstration of how to get ideas without cracking your head open.

For much of my humorous writing I use a simple system of uninspiration. When writing stand-up material for a comedian, for instance, I'll agree some basic themes with the comic, such as divorce, pizza, hotels, and then wander around my home, or around the streets late at night, talking into my tape recorder about divorce, pizza, and hotels, in a bad impersonation of the comedian's voice. An hour's tape will eventually yield, when transcribed and edited, maybe five or ten minutes of material. 'Method writing' you could call it, if you wanted to make it sound more complicated than it is.

The old A–Z trick rarely fails to produce acceptably humorous articles on any given subject. You're asked, for instance, to do a funny piece on cricket. 'Fine,' you say, 'I'll do an A–Z of Cricket.' Having written the letters of the alphabet down the margin of a sheet of paper, you then write appropriate words alongside each letter. U is for Umpire; L is for Leg; S is for Sledging. Once you've got your list it's fairly easy to come up with gags for each trigger word; satirical or comical definitions are the simplest.

I've used a similar uninspiration technique to get me started when writing jokes for greetings cards, listing fifty words to do with, say, Christmas – reindeer, chimneys, divorce – and then mixing them up, looking at them backwards, seeing how the images they invoke can be teased out of cliché and into humour. I used to write spoof quizzes for the comic *Oink!*, one of the most enjoyable jobs I've ever had, and found with them that once I'd come up with the basic format, the stuff would more or less write itself under its own momentum.

And what works for comedy will, at least as far as basic principles, work for most other kinds of writing.

Having ideas is easy. Stopping having them is hard.

Freelances have no absolute time off. If you're away from the forge, you can't make horseshoes. If you're away from the computer, you can always jot yourself a note. And eventually, you see, this will drive you mad and kill you. Yes it will. Ask any doctor. (Well not *any* doctor, obviously. Be fair, ask a doctor who agrees with me.)

Getting stuff finished is the key to progress. For many years I had a thousand and one projects on the go at once, endlessly making notes on this book or that article, writing a paragraph here or a line of dialogue there. Opening new files. Combining old files. Weeding ex-files. My first solo book was published in 1995. I'd started it in about 1980, and it had been awaiting its final edit since at least 1990.

I could do a whole day's work, a whole week's work, and have nothing sellable at the end of it.

Ideas, you see. Ideas are the freelance's albatross. (I think it's albatross; could be aubergine. I'll check later.) If you're any sort of writer, you have a million ideas a day, and you don't want to waste any of them, you want to get them all down, salt them away and sort them away and do something with them before some other bugger beats you to it.

It'll drive you mad. It will.

It used to drive me mad, every time I went down to my allotment to get away from the buzz buzz buzzing bastard bloody idea-flies, they'd follow me. Or another swarm of them would find me, and I'd be up to my elbows in mud and thistles with idea-flies nipping at my ears and I'd have to try and memorise this brilliant snatch of clever talk or mind-twisting plot until I got home. It was like when you're a kid, desperate for a pee, running home with a message for your mum running through your brain. And forgetting it as soon as you reach the gate.

Eventually I discovered an ideas prophylactic which works well for me. It's only this: I always carry a mini tape recorder with me, wherever I go. The allotment, the bath, the pub. I am never without the means to note down my ideas, and consequently I have stopped having ideas at inconvenient moments. My idea incontinence is cured. It's one of those Sod's Law things, you know.

This method might work for you, or you might be able to come up with something else. But whatever you do, you must avoid having too many ideas, or else the ideas will kill you. Even worse, you'll die with all your books, articles and scripts unfinished, so nobody'll ever know what a genius you were.

Homilists are keen on the idea that 'you make your own luck', but it's not like *Blue Peter* – they don't tell you how many egg boxes you're going to need or where to stick your sticky-

OPPORTUNITY SUCKS

back plastic. People who say 'you make your own luck' are usually people who have reached a position of some eminence, at least in their own eyes, and who are reluctant to admit, especially to themselves, that luck got them where they are at least as much as hard work, genius or perseverance.

Hear me now, young ones: luck is *everything*. Or, to be less dramatic about it, luck is the *sine qua non*: luck without talent will see you through, but talent without luck will never earn you a penny piece.

1985 was the year everything changed for me. In the early spring, I wrote a spoof diary column for *The Listener*, and sent it in with a covering letter saying something like 'You always have boring famous people writing the 'Langham Diary'; why don't you let a boring unknown person have a go?'.

I really wanted to write for *The Listener*, more than I've ever wanted just about anything in the writing line. I'd been reading that unique weekly since childhood. I loved its dull design, its musty smell, its dry wit. I loved the fact that it had contributors with names like Wilfred D'eath, and the way it epitomised that strange aspect of British culture which can combine joyful elitism with absolute egalitarianism to create a sort of non-exclusive Shadow Establishment. I loved the way the paper it was printed on went brown almost before you'd got it home from the newsagent.

It's still my idea of what a magazine should sound like and taste like. Like Radio 4 and the World Service, from which it took many of its contents, *The Listener* was full of little corners and unexpected alleys, which led to hidden courtyards in which odd ideas and characters lingered over glasses of calvados in the autumn sun, waiting for a fellow expat from the Planet Interested to wander by and pause for a chat and a smoke.

It's no wonder *The Listener* didn't survive the 1980s. That decade's orthodoxy of surrender could never have been established while such centres of resistance continued. There is a particular kind of nostalgia which is an explosively powerful, and largely unrecognised, force for revolutionary change. If we could only analyse it and synthesise it we could sweep away the old order in days.

Besides which, getting into *The Listener* never did anyone's career any harm. So a couple of weeks after my first mock diary, I sent them another one. I was being stupid, I realise that now; the idea of the undiscovered young talent who draws himself to the attention of the mighty by writing cheeky come-ons which remind them of their own spirituous younger days is a romantic myth. It is unsystematic, idealistic, and lazy.

It worked, obviously, as you'll have gathered from the above build-up. Before my second submission had even had time to reach the magazine, the editor's assistant rang to say that next week's diarist had let them down, and could I stand in?

I got up early the day my 'Langham Diary' came out. I bought a copy of the paper at the stall next to the Underground station. I stood to one side to let the commuters pass me by while I checked the contents list. I was in the contents list. My hands shaking slightly, I turned to the page indicated in the contents list, because contents lists aren't proof positive, they could be wrong. My name was at the top of that page. But I had a quick look at the text below even so, because you never know – they might have put my name there by accident over someone else's stuff.

I was there. My name, my stuff, my thoughts, my name, and my name. I couldn't believe it, I mean that I literally *could not believe it* for quite a few minutes, that something had actually happened for once that was meant to happen; that something so important had gone right.

My first big break.

I passed the train journey to work in the company of a bloke from the pub, a very nice and fantastically boring newlywed, who told me about his DIY. He must have thought I fancied him, the way I nodded and smiled and laughed and hugged myself in apparent response to his adventures with bookshelves and kitchen units and loft insulation. Especially loft insulation – I nearly pissed myself laughing about the loft insulation. At work, during the tea break, a chap from another department said quietly as we passed at the urn, 'Very funny piece in *The Listener* today, did you see?' I blushed and laughed again.

Luck enough there is, and plain for all to see, in the above account. But 1985 wasn't finished with me yet.

A friend of mine had the opportunity to interview Freddie Ross Hancock, who had been Tony Hancock's publicist and second wife. My friend very kindly invited me to accompany him to the interview, at the British Film Institute.

I won't describe that evening in detail, because I wouldn't want you coming over all jealous at all the glamorous people I rubbed elbows with and the legendary top people's hang-out we went onto afterwards and so on, so I'll just say a good time was had by all. Well, by me, anyway.

I cadged a lift home with a BBC radio producer who happened to be amongst those present, and, when the journey was nearly done, I finally dredged up the bottle from somewhere to ask him if, since he'd said he was working on a brand new magazine programme, whether he was at all sort of you know I don't suppose you are but kind of thing do you ever what I'm saying is would it be a complete waste of time like I imagine you get fed up people asking you this but are you interested in ideas from freelances?

Yes, he said.

Oh right, I said. Anywhere along here'll be fine. Thanks for the lift.

The next morning before work I thought up three ideas, typed them up separately on three single sides of A4, and sent them off. That was September. In January – Week One, according to the BBC's internal calendar – I was amongst the contributors to the first edition of a new Radio 4 magazine show. I gave in half my notice at work (went half-time, I mean, on a job share). Lucky, or what? No *what* about it: lucky. Right time, right place, right face. I had no contacts, no background, no particular skills, and yet there I was – half a professional freelance writer and broadcaster.

I'm banging this point home – that there is no 'way in' without the extraordinary strokes of happenstance which it is impossible to plan around – because it's something that the HowToWrite industry, for obvious reasons of self-interest, doesn't often mention. You might be very good, very hard-working, very well organised, but if you're ever going to make the transition from someone who manages to place the occasional poem in an underground SF mag to someone who makes a proper living freelancing, then at some time in your life you are going to have to hit a quite incredible piece of good luck; incredible in the sense that you'd never get away with it in fiction.

And there's nothing you can do to make it happen. *You don't make your own luck.* Sticky-back plastic does not enter into it. Yes, you can make sure that you are ready to exploit your lucky break should it appear, by being organised, inventive, flexible, professional, determined and tireless. But you could be all that for the next seventy-three years and it won't do you sod all good, unless you get lucky.

Intelligent people do not trust their livelihoods to the whims of fate. That does go without saying, doesn't it? Or do you have the writing sickness so badly that you're skipping through these pages, muttering 'When's he going to get onto the bit about SAEs and market research?'.

Being half a library assistant and half a freelance writer and broadcaster was an odd, and slightly uncomfortable experience. But before I could use it as the basis for my first un-published novel, it ended.

I read a piece in a newspaper in which an award-winning young London journalist was getting paid to worry about the lack of upcoming award-winning young journalists in London. He knew personally, he said, of several editors who were actively searching for new writers and were unable to find them.

Bollards, I thought. When was there ever a shortage of would-be writers? Still, no harm in calling his bluff. I wrote to him – there and then, because I assumed that he would get letters from millions of pathetic idiots like me, and I wanted to get in first, before his patience snapped or his postman retired, disabled – asking him, very nicely, to please name names.

(OK, so this one does involve a little bit of sticky-back plastic. But it was still more luck than judgement, you must admit.)

The award-winning young journalist, very nicely, wrote back, in the SAE I had provided (*ah-ha!*), and named one name, that of a section editor at the *London Evening Standard* (as I think it was then called; the *Standard* used to change its name more often than the Liberal Party). I wrote to her, enclosing (*yes*, an SAE obviously, but *also*) a lively covering letter, and my cuttings – which consisted at that time of a few darts humour columns and my 'Langham Diary' from *The Listener*. I thought of enclosing a programme listing from the *Radio Times* with my name underlined, but eventually decided against it.

On the day of the local elections in 1986, my bedsit was being used as a committee room for the forces of progress, when the phone rang and the *Evening Standard* asked me if I fancied interviewing a woman who'd opened a shop selling *Dr Who* memorabilia. I did fancy it. I've still got the badge. Probably worth something by now; you never know.

In at the BBC and in at Fleet Street (that's humour, by the way, not boasting), I could no longer afford the time to work in public libraries, so I left. I was now a full-time freelance writer and broadcaster.

And you can see how I got there now, can't you? You can see how I planned it carefully at every stage, how I followed my plan like a military operation, how my strategic brilliance enabled me to breach the walls of –

The sad thing is, some of you probably *do* think that what I have described above is some sort of blueprint for breaking in. That if you were only to hang around the British Film Institute for a few months, eventually you'd be sure to meet a radio producer who just happened to be starting up a new show, and . . .

Look, I'm going to try once more, and then to hell with you. Here's an analogy. Or simile, or fable, or one of those things. Have you ever wondered why, when mankind can put a man on the moon, cure smallpox and produce computers smaller than matchboxes, half the cricket matches scheduled in this country never take place?

It's because weather, like luck, is something that *happens*. You don't make your own.

HOW TO BE A WOULD-BE WRITER FOREVER

'Euphemism' is, as you know, a euphemism for 'lie'. For example, in America, unpublished, would-be writers are called 'pre-published writers', which is wrong, as well as irritating, since most of them never will be published.

The correct route to writing success is going to Oxford or Cambridge university, being related to someone in the business, and so on. It's not guaranteed, but – well, actually, it *is* guaranteed, provided the world doesn't come to an end, and provided the entire class system doesn't come crashing down around us, which it could, actually, at any moment, so bear that in mind, too; you'd have to be an idiot not to realise today of all days that capitalism most surely does contain the seeds of its own destruction.

But where was I?

Everyone thinks 'I'm socially and emotionally dysfunctional. So why shouldn't I be an artist?'. I reckon about fifty per cent of all the people I know are would-be writers, and of that fifty per cent I imagine at least twenty-five per cent have the necessary ability to write successfully.

That's not surprising. Most people can write reasonably well. At school, writing poems, essays and stories is one of those soft, skivey subjects, usually taught by teachers who've already had nervous breakdowns. It's one of the first activities they set you to when you start school, because it's something that even tiny tots can manage, unlike, say, chemistry or Russian or even PE. Writing isn't difficult. It isn't brain surgery, it isn't music, it isn't assembling flat-pack furniture.

Ah. But of all those friends and acquaintances of mine who think they could write, *should* write, have a right to write, it goes without saying that hardly any of them ever will write. Not because they can't, but (and I apologise if I'm getting a bit too untechnical here) because they won't.

The only really significant difference between those who want to do it and do it, and those who want to do it and don't do it, is that those who want to do it and do it do it, whereas those who want to do it and don't do it don't do it.

I know that sounds ridiculously simple, but it is all the difference in the world. Those who want to write but don't write will die still wanting to write and still not having written. If you haven't got what it takes to bloody well get down and bloody well do it – and it doesn't take much, for heaven's sake, just the ability to sit in a chair and type for half an hour a day – then forget about talent, you might as well stop reading now and get yourself another hobby.

Would-be writers – 'wouldys' – must be the stupidest, maddest group of people in the world, even compared to all other hobbies, interest groups, religious and political brotherhoods and so on.

If – heaven forbid – someone found a way to assemble a thousand wouldys in one place at one time, you would have there the highest concentration of mental feebleness, emotional disability and defective personality ever gathered together.

I once met a man who edited a technical newsletter of some sort. It consisted of about ten stapled pages, produced once a week, full of esoteric numbers and diagrams – something to do with the financial markets, I believe. It cost a fortune to subscribe to, and its subscription list was deliberately restricted. It did not appear in any writers' market book or listing, because it did not use any writers.

And yet, this bloke insisted, there had never been a week since he took over the editorship that he hadn't received at least one postal submission of a batch of poems.

Isn't that incredible? What makes it so amazing is not merely that the world is so full of unhinged would-be writers, but that, unhinged though they are, they posses the resources to track down this obscure, unlisted periodical in order to send it their poetry. They are capable of that impressive feat of detection – and yet they are incapable of carrying out the tiniest, most basic act of market research which would have told them that *Boring Numbers Weekly* did not publish verse!

Or then again, maybe they knew perfectly well what kind of publication it was. Certainly, there are wouldys who seem to believe that their work has a kind of mystical force; that all they need to do is keep sending the stuff out, to anyone who is foolish enough to possess a postal address, and sooner or later their undoubted genius will be discovered.

Mad people. Mad and stupid and a complete waste of space. Still – as long as it keeps 'em happy, eh?

I ran a fanzine for a while, and this was at a time when various social and technological factors were conspiring to wobblify the boundaries between fanzines and small press and prozines, so I sent the magazine's details to the writers' mags, inviting writers to send for my contributor's guidelines.

The idea, obviously, was that people would buy my fanzine in order to find out how to write for it. And they did, so in that respect I was farsighted and wise. What I hadn't worked out was that if you give your address to a lot of would-be writers, you will very soon be knee-deep in loony crap.

Loony, loony, loony crap.

I have to be careful here, because for all I know some of these nuts might still be alive – though I doubt whether any of them ever read anything except market newsletters ('*Crochet Weekly* offers a small paper bag as first prize to the sender of its Star Letter'). There's one letter in particular from a wouldy that I have kept all these years, because I couldn't believe it when it arrived and I can't believe it now, over a decade later. When pals come round for a drink and a giggle, I get this letter out and show it to them, along with my John Stonehouse autograph.

First let me explain what my magazine was about. It was called *The Comedy Magazine* and it was about comedy. I had wanted to start a comedy fanzine since the mid-1970s, and finally succeeded in doing so in the mid-80s. TCM ran for two issues; one more than most fanzines. Since then there have been many comedy magazines in the UK, none of them much more successful than mine, but at the time, the idea was very unfamiliar.

No matter how clear I tried to make my writer's guidelines ('It's a magazine about comedy. It contains interviews, reviews and features. It does not contain jokes, sketches or other funny material. It is not in the market for features on tropical fish. Strictly no poetry'), I still received pages of jokes, limericks, anecdotes and . . .

My favourite. Handwritten in block capitals throughout, except for the sender's name, which was illegible. On both sides of a single sheet of lined blue writing paper it offered me 'details of personalities of vintage dance band leaders, written in the 1934–5 era', a snippet from a 1935 gossip column, and a joke about a courting couple in a dance hall: 'Ted Heath told me that one. I wonder if he remembers'.

And right at the end, the inevitable: 'I am an OAP'.

Well of course you are, dear. I could have told *you* that. Why else would you be reading a writer's magazine?

Too late for Ted Heath's mate, but the rest of us would do well to remember that if you ever write something which you feel must be accompanied by an excuse or plea in mitigation – 'I am an OAP' – 'Sorry if it seems a bit rushed but I've only got a week to live' – then don't send it in.

'I know it's not very good but I am just starting out and need a bit of encouragement'.

There are editors reading this now, nodding their heads, grinding their teeth, saying 'Yup, I've seen that one, too'.

Of course all this gives a bad reputation to the few sane would-be writers – there's always got to be a large majority, hasn't there, who ruin it for everyone else?

HOW TO GIVE A COMPETITION JUDGE A BELLY LAUGH

I don't remember every cheque I've ever received, but some stick in the memory. Sixty-two pounds and fifty pence – that's one I'll never forget, because at the time I received it it was by far the biggest writing cheque I'd ever had, and because it was payment for a short poem which had probably taken me about ten minutes to write. And because I employed more skill in the earning of that £62.50 than I did in the writing of the poem.

It was joint first prize (hence the odd sum) in the under-25 section of a national CND poetry competition. I couldn't get the Saturday off work to travel up North for the presentation, so the CND sent me my little trophy through the post (it arrived slightly shattered; if you want a Cold War analogy at this point, could you kindly supply your own? I'm busy). The poem was printed on page two of the *Morning Star*. I daresay there are still verse fans in Minsk and Moscow who, when in their cups, recite chunks of 'The Dust Under My Bed' by grett pote ov Inglitch ravilootion, Kumraid Mit Kart.

I entered that competition with the intention of winning money. I was a CND member, though not particularly a lover of poetry, but it was the money that excited me – that, and the name of one of the judges: Roger McGough.

I did enjoy the poetry of McGough and his fellow Mersey Beaters, and, more importantly, I felt that his was a style in which I could write. I asked myself 'What will be the predominant voice of the works submitted to a CND poetry competition?' and I answered 'Predominately, they will be soppy, angry, humourless, and full of images of doves, mushroom clouds and innocent babies'.

So, I thought, is this sort of thing likely to appeal to a Merseyside maverick, a scansion scally, like old Rog? Or would he prefer to read something modern in form, bittersweet in content, and colloquial in style, adorned with mundane references and daft jokes as counterpoints to the high-minded universality of the closing lines?

I didn't bother answering. I know a rhetorical question when I ask myself one.

Sixty-two pounds fifty, eh? Not bad. I worked it out as an hourly rate and realised that for those few minutes I had been earning more than my boss's boss.

I've entered quite a few competitions over the years, and had the odd success. I've tended not to go in for ones that charge entry fees, but only because I've always been short of money. If you've got a well-paid day job, then why not? I see nothing wrong with entry fees in principle.

Competitions can help get you used to writing to deadline, to a certain length and on a specific subject. At worst, you will end up with a completed piece of work which you might be able to use elsewhere. At best, you could walk away with £62.50 and a slightly shattered trophy.

It was only when I crossed the road, however, and started *judging* the occasional competition, that I realised how easy it ought to be to win the first prize every time, given that almost all of the entries are, to use a technical term, utter snot. Opening my first bundle of short stories as a competition judge was one of the most depressing moments of my life.

At least half of the stories were very obviously bottom-drawer rejects, which had no connection whatsoever to the (quite specific) theme of the competition. Some had tried to get round this slight problem by inserting – *in biro* – the odd key word here and there throughout the script.

One man sent in a personal memoir of his idyllic Lake District childhood. Not only had he ignored the theme, he hadn't even made the tiniest attempt to fictionalise the piece; the main 'character' bore the author's name, and at the end this genius had added a handwritten note: 'This is all true, by the way'.

At first, I thought I was seeing a lot of stream-of-consciousness stories, but after a while I realised it wasn't that at all, it was just that these people were incapable of making sense for more than three or four words at a time.

Several stories did adhere to the competition's theme, but were GCSE-type essays, not stories: 'On the one hand, we might say . . . and in conclusion, we see how . . .'

There was what almost seemed to be a deliberate conspiracy to avoid using any imagination. The stories were so bloody obvious, so old hat, so numbingly trite. They came straight from Shakespeare, or the Bible, or 1950s horror comics. Most of the competitors were clearly people who hadn't read a short story since their schooldays, forty years earlier. I would estimate that about 80% of the stories were identical, in plot and in manner of telling. And *that* story wasn't even a good one!

Presentation was unbelievable. Competitors with access to wordprocessors had decorated their manuscripts with all manner of ornate typefaces and curly bits, and yet hardly any of the entries seemed to have been read through, even once, before posting. Sentences with missing words were common, and even those who'd used spellchecking facilities were prone to spelling 'god' as 'dog' and 'car' as 'cat'. Interestingly, the older writers (yes, a lot of them put their age on the title page; and no, I don't know why, either) were generally worse at spelling and basic grammar than the younger ones.

Very quickly, I got to the point where I could tell how awful a story would be just by glancing at the way it was presented. I could have been wrong, of course – and I always read on carefully, to make sure I wasn't – but I never was. Not once. The better stories, without exception, were decently typed, and tended not to have whole sections crossed out and rewritten in the margins along with the pencilled note 'Sorry! Ignore this!'.

For reasons which, I suspect, only a psychologist could properly explain, an infallible guide to badness was the indentation at the beginning of paragraphs. The more spaces, and the more variation from one paragraph to another, the more crap the story; the more bonkers the author.

The worst part of the whole ordeal, though, was when they tried to be funny. I'm not even going to talk about that. I'm serious. It was so painful – so physically painful – that I just don't want to think about it. You wouldn't let an amateur loose on your mouth with a dental drill, would you? And yet in this so-called civilised society anyone who feels like it is permitted to set themselves up as a humorous writer. It's madness!

Anyway, there you go, that lot was better out than in. But just think, next time you enter a short-story competition and don't win a prize: your story must have been really, really bad if it didn't even come in the top three. *Really* bad.

One of the best methods of early failure is premature success.

SUCCESS = FAILURE

I sold my first book when I was 23. I was paid a £50 advance for it, which I'm glad to say I didn't have to pay back when the book was cancelled, because if I had had to pay it back I would probably have gone to prison since there was never a period of 48 hours in those days when I had fifty pounds in liquidatable assets.

I don't want to go into too much detail about this, because it was a fairly painful episode and one I don't care to think about a lot.

Besides, they might want their fifty quid back.

The brief version is this. I had an idea for a book on a subject which was then of great personal significance. I wrote an outline, and sent it to the only publisher who was at all likely to accept it. That publisher turned it down, in a friendly and detailed letter. So far, so everyday story of writing fools, but here's where I made my big mistake.

I replied to the commissioning editor's letter, meeting every point he'd raised with a fresh argument, and modifying my original proposal to fit in with his objections. He was so impressed by my youthful exuberance, my obvious commitment and my dialectic skills, that he asked me to come and see him and his colleague to discuss the project further.

That meeting ended with them commissioning the book, and so began the worst year of my life. You remember when you were little and burping and your gran used to say you had eyes bigger than your belly?

My original book proposal would have been fairly easy to write, and would have worked as a book. Whether it would have worked as a product from the publisher's point of view, I can't say. But the version of the project which was commissioned was bloody murder to write, and didn't work as a book, and I knew it wouldn't right from the start.

The thing is, I was too good a salesman. The publishers were surely right to turn me down in the first place, and shouldn't have let themselves be talked round by a mouthy kid.

They were as much to blame as I was, which is why I felt fine about keeping their fifty quid. I was so carried away by the growing realisation that I *could* talk them round, that I allowed myself to talk myself into agreeing to write a bastardised version of my book in which I had no confidence, and little interest.

You know, 'because it was there' and all that.

I learned my lesson: don't believe your own propaganda, don't sell anything you don't know you can write, don't fall for the idea that ambition is a good thing. Don't have eyes bigger than your belly.

The miracle is that that experience, that dreadful, slogging year of writing a book I knew wasn't what the publishers wanted, didn't put me off writing for life. Let's hope that you have better luck: that you undergo a similar experience, but that it scars you so horribly that you renounce writing forever. That way you won't have to read the rest of this book.

HOW TO DIE

A few years after I became a full-time freelance, a health problem which I'd had for a while suddenly turned much worse. It wasn't (it still isn't) a very serious illness, but it did have the unfortunate effect of keeping me pretty much within the boundaries of my own home and my own company.

At first, this didn't matter a great deal. I was going through one of my occasional successful periods at that time (successful by my standards, that is; meaning I was able to pay my utility bills by cheque instead of by credit card). Although I wasn't getting out and about, people I had seen in the previous month, or six months, or year still had me in their minds. When opportunities came up they would still, sometimes, think of me (although not necessarily first – and what they thought of me in connection with wouldn't necessarily be something I would rather do than die).

Even the fact that I was unable to attend meetings wasn't automatically fatal to my involvement in a project. Almost all meetings are unnecessary, in any field of human endeavour, and almost all human endeavourers recognise this, if only at a subconscious level.

Certainly, my apparent conversion to the hermitic lifestyle caused some puzzlement amongst my business contacts – though I should say that such puzzlement was not entirely their fault. I soon learned that if you tell someone 'I can't come into London and have lunch with you next Tuesday because I'm not well', they will very rarely believe you; more than that, they won't even bother disbelieving you, assuming instead that your illness is a polite, or maybe even rude, fiction – assuming, in other words, that you don't *intend* them to take your words literally. Don't ask me why (I think I could probably tell you, in fact, but it would take another book as long as this one to do so); the point is that after a while I stopped telling people that I couldn't go and see them because I couldn't travel, and simply told them that I was too busy. There, let them pick the bones out of that.

And some took offence, and some didn't. And some, undoubtedly, exhaled big gusts of relief as soon as they were off the phone, having only asked me to come in and see them because that was what custom and practice demanded and not because they especially wanted to waste yet another two or three hours in the company of yet another embittered, gauche, socially maladjusted writer whose entire conversation would consist of whinging on about small fees and late payments and vandalising subs and two-faced editors and people who don't return phone calls . . .

Anyway, as I say, it all seemed to work out for a time, and I even began to sort of think that maybe I'd kind of got away with it.

A self-employed person who gets away with being ill? Come on, boy, wake up!

Eventually, after something like three or four years, my income suffered a significant decline which was to a large extent directly attributable to a decline in my business's stock of goodwill.

What I learned from this was that acquaintanceship requires frequent reinforcement. Friendship is different: I have friends I haven't seen for twenty years, and they're still friends. (Especially those who I know for sure are still alive.) In fact, if I never see them, they're more likely to remain friends, because there is less opportunity to fall out with them.

But acquaintances . . . they forget. The memory of that lunch they had with you, the one where you were so witty, and flirted so charmingly, and seemed so full of brilliant ideas and daring plans and exciting projects . . . it fades. Your face fades. Your voice fades. Your place in their limited memory capacity is taken by newer acquaintances.

They haven't got it in for you; they haven't turned against you; it's just that, when they need someone to write the ad libs for their star client's latest chat show, you're not at the front of their minds, so they don't think of you first. Or second. Or third. And the fourth guy they phone says 'Yes'.

What I should have done, when I started to get ill, is get a job. A proper, regular, dull day job, with paid sick leave, pension plan, maybe even a company doctor. That is definitely what I should have done.

Of course, getting ill is not something you can avoid. (Apologies to those of you who make a living writing books called *Think Yourself Slim!* or *Stop Smoking, Start Living!* or *Fart Your Way To Immortality!* but it isn't; it just isn't. Illness is random, off the record, non-attributable. The only thing we know for sure that causes illness is poverty – and poverty, whatever you may have been told at school if you were educated during the last twenty years, is never the fault of the poor.)

On the other hand, you might be lucky and get an early warning that you are about to be boarded by a chronic, non-fatal, career-shafting condition. If you do receive that early warning, then please take my sincere, urgent, hard-mined advice: *get a job, Nob.* If you possibly can, shield yourself behind an employer who is going to have to pay you a pension if he sacks you for being sick.

I didn't, and by the time I realised what was happening, it was far too late for me to get employed. What I did instead was start from something like ground zero. Start again as a writer, working mostly in areas, and for people, who didn't know me, and who therefore knew me from the start of our relationship as someone who didn't attend meetings, didn't go to lunch, didn't exist except via post, email and phone. I also moved from London to Somerset around this time, which didn't hurt; everyone in London knows that you can't get to London from anywhere else in the UK except via New York or Paris.

They may have thought I was eccentric, but at least they didn't see me change; at least they didn't take it personally.

Not long after Margaret Thatcher's third and most hideous election victory, I was invited to write some links for a children's TV series. The presenter was a comic I'd worked with before, and the 'links' were the little bits of monologue and dialogue separating the items on the shows.

It wasn't a bad job, steady money for a few weeks, and it's lucky I'd already got the gig before the producer asked me for my fax number. 'Fax?' I replied, as if the word were one I'd barely heard of.

Which, in fact, it was. I'd never heard of a private individual owning a fax machine; I'd never worked in an office where there was a fax machine; I'd never even *seen* a fax machine, except on telly.

It was an embarrassing situation. Once a week, the show's running order would be biked to my home in the suburbs, I would write my links, and then another bike messenger would pick them up and rush them back to the studio. Heaven knows how much of the programme's budget was wasted on couriers, all for the want of what the producer clearly considered a basic piece of equipment.

Needless to say, the first thing I bought with my fee from that job was a fax machine. And as soon as I was able to, I had an extra phone line put in, so that when people wanted to send me a fax I no longer had to tell them to ring off, wait a few minutes while I unplugged the phone and plugged in the fax, and then dial again.

I was the same with computers. I wasted any amount of money on electronic typewriters which kept going wrong before I was finally persuaded to buy my first wordprocessor, and it wasn't until years later that I eventually upgraded to a proper computer – not until the day that I needed to send a book manuscript on disc to a publisher and found that I was the only person in the English-speaking world who still used Amstrad discs, which were expensively incompatible with all other makes.

I don't like technology. I don't know many writers who do. The only thing about fancy equipment which you can be absolutely certain of is that sooner or later it will break down, and that when it does it will cause an almost unbelievable amount of chaos in your life.

If I could get away with it, I'd still write on a manual typewriter, and send my work out by pigeon. But I can't get away with it, and that's my point.

Yes, there are still professional writers who type their novels, or even write them in longhand. But they are not people like you and me: they are stars. They can do what they want, because they're valuable properties, worth fussing over, worth – from a publisher's point of view – the extra trouble and expense.

If you run a biscuit factory, you have to make sure that your plant is at least as up-to-date as that employed by your rivals, and the same is true for writers.

The very first bit of Boy Wonder's Ace Writing Kit I ever bought was a telephone answering machine, and I'll tell you why I bought it. I bought it because my girlfriend and I, who did not live together, both worked shifts. Before I had the machine installed, I would have to wait by my phone every evening for her to ring me so that I knew that she had got home safely, so that I could go out to the pub with a clear conscience.

That's why I spent the rent money on an answering machine; so that I could go boozing straight from work, and use my remote control interrogator to check on my girlfriend's safe return.

For the first, and almost certainly last time in my life I was a high tech pioneer. The only person my friends and I knew of who had an answering machine was the private eye Jim Rockford, and he of course was a fictional character. (One of my tragically few claims to fame is that I was, I honestly believe, the first person in this country to call the bleeps 'bleeps' instead of 'the tone'; as in 'Please leave a message after the bleeps'.)

When I started getting serious about freelancing, it came as a mild surprise to me to discover that my Rockford machine had business uses as well as social ones.

Nowadays, obviously, it would be impossible to imagine operating as a freelance writer without using an answering machine; apart from anything else, you'd have to talk to everyone who rang you. It is as indispensable as a pocket cassette recorder, or as the telephone itself.

Apart from the fact that you absolutely must have one, the only really useful piece of advice I have concerning answering machines is *don't record a humorous outgoing message*. Not only because all decent people find humorous outgoing messages deeply irritating, but also because (and I've told this story elsewhere, probably more than once, so please skip it if it begins to feel familiar) humour is not appropriate to absolutely all situations. I once heard of man whose outgoing message was about a minute long, and consisted of funny voices, classic comedy samplings, celebrity soundalikes and wacky screams, climaxing in several seconds of echo-effect farting noises. And one late night he arrived home to discover just one message waiting for him: 'John, this is Mum. Can you ring home urgently please? It's your father . . . [caller's voice obscured by sobbing] . . . The policeman said he was dead long before they managed to shift the horse . . . '

(Second thoughts, those of you who did skip that, you might want to go back and read it. I told it much better this time, added some really neat details, eg farting noises and a horse. Give it a go, see what you think.)

Nowadays, of course, my fax machine rarely bleeps, as almost all my business is done by email. I wasn't exactly an early-adopter of that, either, though I did get the message in the end. For some months, I was aware of the slight note of astonished contempt in editors' voices when they said 'Could you email that to me?' and I'd say 'Well, no, not really, but I could fax it'.

'Fax?' they'd reply, as if the word were one they'd barely heard of.

Joke. Sorry. Poor taste.

REVEALED: THE SECRETS OF HOW TO HAVE A SUCCESSFUL CAREER AS A WRITER

3: Editors and other enemies

HOW TO INTERROGATE AN EDITOR

When an editor commissions a piece of writing from you, it is your job to find out what he wants, not his job to tell you. Seems odd, I know, but that's how it works. Editors never know what they want. They are busy people, they don't have time to know what they want. All they know is that they have an article-shaped hole on one of their pages, and that they want you to fill it.

The following is a transcript of a telephone call with an editor. I've changed the details to protect the poor idiot's identity.

ED: . . . anyway, we're doing this like special sort of, y'know, on bananas, and I was thinking how about like, doing a thing?

ME: Who, me?

ED: Yeah, y'know, right.

ME: You want me to write a piece for your special issue on bananas?

ED: So what do you think? Hold on . . . John says what's the score because the teletext's not working.

ME: 14 for 3, last I heard. So you –

ED: Hold on . . . John says is that England?

ME: Of course it's bloody England! What does it sound like, South Africa?

ED: Yeah, John, that's England. So, what you reckon, you up for that?

ME: You talking to me? Yeah, sure, I'm up for that. Just let me get a few details . . .

ED: I'm going to have to go in a minute, John's got a –

ME: Yeah, but let me just check I've got this. What sort of, like, y'know, piece are you looking for, for a start? Do you know what I mean?

ED: Yeah, you know, just one of your usual things.

ME: You want a humour piece?

ED: Sure, you know, one of your Specials. Like, with extra capers.

ME: OK, so –

ED: Four cheeses. Hold the garlic.

ME: OK, so –

ED: I'm going to have to go . . .

ME: No, hold on – are you still there? You still there? Listen, just give me a key word, yeah? Are we after satire here? Wacky? Jokey? Um . . . are you still there? Corny? Filthy? Topical? Sceptical? Dental?

ED: Sceptical, right. That'll be great. I've got to –

ME: *Sceptical?* What, definitely?

ED: Right.

ME: And funny?

ED: Right.

ME: About bananas. OK, no prob. Now – how many words?

ED: Oh, give me a break! Whatever's, you know . . .

ME: Just roughly. *Please*, just give me a vague, you know, a hint. A nod. A million words? Less than a million? Come on –

ED: Say, third of a page. You know the page size we use for our specials?

ME: So how many words is that? Roughly?

ED: Oh God . . . hold on . . .

ME: OK, no, OK, forget that. Deadline: when do you need it?

ED: Ahhhhh . . . pretty soon. Soon as you can, really.

ME: OK, OK. What about the money? What can you pay for this?

ED: Listen, I gotta go, really. Call me tomorrow . . .

I should add that, although editors may not know what they want when they commission it, by the time you've delivered the piece they have often miraculously discovered what it was that they wanted and, like, y'know, what you've written wasn't exactly, sort of, y'know, exactly what they had in mind, kinda thing . . .

Another irritating habit which many editors have – particularly busy ones, working for big organisations – is not making negative responses: they tell you if they've accepted a piece, but if they reject it you never hear from them. The opposite annoyance – when an editor uses your submission without telling you – is also fairly common, so make sure you keep an eye on any title to which you've submitted work.

This is inconvenient, frustrating, rude, unprofessional and inefficient. But it's life. This problem has only a partial solution: the withdrawal letter, well known to small press writers. After waiting a sensible amount of time to allow the editor to reply (take the number of weeks you first thought of, double it, and then wait another month), you write again, in friendly tones, and enclosing another SAE, asking for a decision, and adding that, if you haven't heard back within a month, you'll assume the answer's no and submit the piece elsewhere. A month later, you write again (still friendly, but no SAE this time), formally withdrawing the item.

This approach isn't infallible: editors don't often read letters from contributors, and are quite capable of using the piece a year later – embarrassing in the unlikely event that you really have sold it elsewhere in the meantime. There's nothing you can do about that, except hope that editor B doesn't read editor A's magazine, and if he does, and complains to you, badmouth A to B. Oh yes, and make sure you get paid by both of them.

TURN THAT THING DOWN!

There's a story about an ultra-professional old penny-a-word fiction freelance, a man who answered with pride to the name of Jack Hack, who got a call one day from an editor he'd worked for many times before.

'Jack,' says the editor, 'you've gotta help me, man, I'm in a hole. I'm putting together this cowboy anthology, and one of my big name writers has let me down at the last minute. I need a 7,000 word all-action oater, and I need it on my desk by Tuesday. Can you do it?'

The writer says sure, no problem, because that's what he always says. He's made a living for a long time by saying 'Sure, no problem' to editors.

'Great!' says the editor. 'You've saved my life, Jack, no kidding. Oh, incidentally – you are familiar with the genre, right? I mean, like, have you ever actually read a Western story?'

To which the hack replies, rather haughtily: 'Read one? My dear boy, I've never even *written* one.'

Jack's approach is the traditional one, but it's not the only one. Sometimes, in my opinion, you just have to say 'No'.

A very silly woman from *The Oldie* magazine once rang me in a very silly state of excitement, after reading a short piece I'd had in another magazine (that's all these magazine people do all day, honestly; read each other's mags and look for things to nick). This was definitely the funniest thing she'd ever read in her life, or at least since she got back from lunch, and how about turning it into a series for her? Well, yeah, fine. How about that. Actually, it sounded a pretty lame idea to me, but if she wanted to pay for it – hey, no skin off my pyjamas.

Her 'idea' was, as always, a nebulous non-starter, but I spent a few hours on it, and she liked what I'd done and asked me to do some more, so I spent more hours on it, and . . . and, well, obviously, in the end nothing happened. In fact, I didn't even get a final 'No' out of her, because by that time she'd left the job. *In fact*, now I come to think of it, I realise for the first time that I must actually have wasted some hours working on her stupid non-idea at the exact same time that she was having her leaving do.

I wonder what her maiden name was. Is it possible that she was that girl whose knickers I pulled down from behind during the school photo when we were six, and that she had been waiting all those years to get even with me?

Mandy, babe – *is that you?*

Editors have stupid ideas. This is like saying horses have big cocks.

Anyway, the next time I got a call from a silly editor with a silly idea, I thought 'No, not this time, I'm going to put my foot down'. I can't remember now what the silly idea was, but it might have been the time a Sunday supplement wanted me to spend the night in a West End hotel, ringing room service every half hour throughout the night to demand things like inflatable women and cocaine and see how the poor underpaid bastard on night duty reacted and then stitch him up in print. Could have been that, couldn't it? Sounds like the sort of thing that might make you say 'No, not this time, I'm going to put my foot down', doesn't it?

If it wasn't that it was some equally embarrassing Oxbridge-flavoured heap of stinking dung, so when she'd finished outlining what she wanted me to do (and how much she was going to pay me: twenty quid plus expenses, the tight cow) I said 'I don't think that'll work'.

Long silence. Followed, without a noticeable break, by another long silence. 'Well,' she said, at last. 'That's *me* told then, isn't it?' I never heard from her again. Perhaps I needed a more subtle approach.

What I do now is, I keep a list of names by my phone. These are 'friends' of mine, people I know in the freelancing business, and I wouldn't be at all surprised to learn that some of them also keep lists of names by their phones or that my name is on some of those lists.

And when an editor rings to say he's just had this brilliant after-lunch idea, right up your street, what it is, is why don't we get you a rubber mask and paint your bottom purple and send you to infiltrate the baboons at London Zoo, I simply reach for my list and say 'Sadly, much as I'd love to get in amongst those primates, nothing I'd like more in fack, but I'm just off to Bulgaria for three weeks on an exchange visit with the video critic of *Tractor* magazine. However, I know who'd be just about perfect for your exciting project, won't even need the mask, and that's my mate Pete. I just happen to have his number right here . . .'

It goes without saying, I trust, that all the above depends on how desperate for work I am at the time. There have been many weeks when my only questions would be 'Does it have to be purple?' and 'Can I put the bananas on expenses?'.

HOW TO GET SUED   HowToWrite books and mags frequently include a few pages on 'Libel Law for Writers – What You Need to Know', usually written by a country solicitor living on the South Coast, who retired fifteen years ago, and who even when he was working only broke from his routine of conveyancing and more conveyancing to do an uncontested divorce about once a year. You know who he is, don't you? He is himself a would-be writer who's been told to 'write what you know'.

And this is supposed to equip you against the most terrifying ordeal a writer can face? Give me strength.

The very idea that writers should know libel law is absurd, for starters. Most lawyers don't know libel law. Most libel lawyers don't know libel law. Libel is a specialism within a specialism within a profession. To say that the poor bloody freelance writer has got to become a libel specialist along with everything else – computer expert, management consultant, salesman, etc etc etc – is to stretch the definition of freelance far too far.

There are, however, certain things you need to know about libel, and the best person to ask about them is probably someone who's been sued and has survived. Me, for instance.

Yeah, baby, I been sued by some real *mothers* in my time, I can tell ya. Man, I been sued by some *cornfed beasts* in my time, and I'm still here to tell the tale. So here's what you need to know, precis style.

1. Contrary to very popular belief, you can't defuse a libel simply by bunging 'allegedly' in front of it. If you write that the leader of the opposition is actually a 104-year-old transsexual who once served as a member of Hitler's personal bodyguard, and then you add 'or so it is rumoured', your clever little disclaimer will prove to be a crash helmet made of custard should you end up being sued.

2. Any decent employer – magazine, paper, radio network – will take the rap for you if you do get sued. Assuming you haven't committed the libel maliciously or wilfully, then it is, after all, more the editor's fault than yours. You are only an ignorant writer, no matter how many articles by retired Bognor solicitors you've read; the editor is presumably trained in excision, and is undeniably responsible for what finally appears in his title. And as I say, most of them are pretty good about this. When I was sued by a former Tory cabinet minister the first I knew of it was when I read about the settlement in a daily newspaper. That suited me fine, and proved that the people I was writing for were good gentlefolk of the old school.

3. Few suings get to court. People sue from various motives. If your magazine has money, then they sue in the hope of winning the fabled 'Jury Lottery'. Or they may sue in order to gain publicity, because their star is dimming with age and the wheel of fashion's endless turnings. Political suings are not unknown, aimed at silencing a dissenting voice. Some sue because what you've said about them is damagingly true, and issuing a writ is their last desperate attempt to convince a sceptical world of their innocence. Occasionally – very, very occasionally – they might even sue because they are outraged by your wicked lies and cannot rest until they have cleared their names. But usually it's the money. And therefore, they will almost always settle out of court.

4. Despite the above, you could get clobbered, it does happen (writs generally name the writer, the editor, the publisher, and sometimes even the distributors and retailers of the allegedly offending item), and as a responsible freelance it is up to you to take sensible precautions, ie make sure everything is in the wife's name. (NB: I refuse to turn this into one of those tedious books which has 'she/ he' or 'hers/his' on every other line. If I tell you to put everything in the wife's name, and you have a husband rather than a wife, then what I'm going to do is, I'm going to make the astonishingly bold assumption that you are in fact intelligent enough to figure out what I mean and to make the necessary adjustments for yourself.)

5. The sued as well as the suing will usually be keen to settle a case without going to court. It's not uncommon for editors to settle even when they are quite certain that they haven't published a libel, and that no jury on earth would believe they had. In the end, it's often cheaper and easier for editors to accept defeat at an early stage (having first tried bluffing the suer with a barrage of lawyers' letters), to publish a small, insincere apology, and to make a token payment to the 'victim'. This is for two main reasons. The first is one which you already know: the libel laws in this country are crazy, disgraceful and thoroughly anti-democratic. You will often hear it said that 'only lawyers win at libel', but this is not the whole truth. In fact, only lawyers and rich people win at libel. Bringing or defending a libel suit is fantastically expensive and time-consuming, which is why, in almost all cases, the victor in a libel trial will be the party with most resources. The truth of the matter is irrelevant. The second reason is this:

6. It is no good a writer trying to figure out from Retired of Bognor's articles what precisely does or does not constitute libel. Almost anything you write about anyone can be libellous, depending on the judge, the jury, the lawyers, the celebrity status of the suer, the prevailing moral climate . . . anything. Most of us, for instance, would argue that, in a democratic society, writers have a duty to be caustically abusive about public figures; but I can think of at least one notorious example of a celebrity successfully suing a newspaper which had done nothing more terrible or unusual than printing nasty remarks about the celebrity's physical appearance. An innocent gag – all right then, a not-so-innocent gag – could ruin you; literally, ruin you, for ever. I would therefore like to take this opportunity to publicly thank the former Home Secretary whose face I once described in print as 'resembling a bottom which had just undergone one of those Cleveland Social Services anal dilation tests'. They may have been rubbish at running the country, them Tories, but at least some of them could take a joke.

7. A decent editor or sub-editor will find a way of allowing you to say what you meant to say without bringing bankruptcy to all that you touch.

Other than that, what can I say? Be careful who you write for, be careful what you say, be careful who you say it about, and try only to libel people who you know to be either desperately poor or dying of a debilitating illness.

And while you're at it, you might have a word with your insurance broker. You never know.

HOW COME THEY CAN'T EVEN SPELL MY NAME RIGHT?

Shortly after the invention of all-day pub opening, a friend and I wrote a humour piece in which most of the jokes depended on misspellings. It was funnier than it sounds, actually. But not, actually, all that much funnier. We didn't work particularly hard on that piece, I have to say; we were doing one of those hot day things that freelances occasionally allow themselves, whereby my mate came over to my place and we went round the pub and drank beer in the beer garden and ate grated cheese sandwiches (the cheese was grated, not the sandwiches) and played the quiz machines and chatted and went 'Christ, is it hot or what?' for the whole of the day until it was the evening and therefore time to go out to the pub anyway, and throughout all that day we *kept a notebook and pen close at hand* and therefore we were working. It was a working day. It just happened to be the sort of working day best spent in the pub.

The following morning, I squinted at the notebook, found it to be in some respects incomplete as far as providing the text of an 800-word humour feature went, and phoned my collaborator. We spent the next half hour expanding on the single joke we had come up with the previous day, and then I wrote it up and faxed it in. It was raining that day; in my view, the ideal weather for a day in the pub, but you see, self-discipline is in a very real sense what this freelancing game is all about.

So, to recap, we wrote a humour piece which depended for its humorous effect on misspellings. And this here is an essay about sub-editors, so if you can guess what comes next, you are only twice as intelligent as you need to be to qualify for Mensa membership.

The sub corrected all our misspellings.

Probably for the first time in his life.

God knows what anyone who happened to read the printed piece would have thought – a piece recognisable by typography, headline, by-line and illustration as a Funny Piece, but which, thanks to the subs, did not contain a single humorous word, thought or deed. Sadly, I suspect what they thought was: 'I see these guys are about as funny as usual. Think I'll do the crossword'.

A few years later I wrote, or compiled, a whole book that consisted of printing errors, double entendres, and the like. You can imagine the fun I had proof reading that for the publishers – though, to her credit, the editor had only managed to 'correct to death' one of the entries.

There was another sub I used to do a bit of stuff for who was always adding terrible jokes to my pieces. If I was doing a bit that included a lot of jokes about, say, dogs, and he thought there were two or three dog jokes that I'd missed, he'd just bung 'em in.

Anyone who has ever written for newspapers or magazines will tell you about MY LIFE OF HELL WITH CRAP SUB HORROR, if you are foolish or charitable enough to give them the opportunity. It is one of the great, grinding, inescapable eternals of the writer's life; it is irritating, frustrating, saddening, maddening, and sometimes troublesome. It has got far worse since Thatcher and Murdoch used systematic violence to smash the print unions at Wapping, thus replacing capable craftsmen with 'multiskilled' (ie unskilled and scared of the dole) teenage journalists, who are computer literate but not literally literate. The old dinosaurs of the print unions were right: once you get rid of craftsmen, you get rid of standards. It really is that simple: the despised 'Spanish practices' lead to classical quality. In order to have a well-printed journal you need several dozen chain-smoking West Ham supporters standing about in a pub on Fleet Street for five or six hours a night getting paid more than the prime minister. I'm not being facetious; this was a tried and tested system which worked, despite what liberal journalists will tell you, until the modernisers came along and destroyed it.

The curse of the subs is . . . well, apart from anything else, it is something that it's very easy to get obsessed with. I don't know how many hundreds or thousands of articles I've had published over the last decade or so, but I doubt if more than a dozen of them have been printed error-free. It's not at all unusual, for instance, for a sub in a hurry who needs to save a couple of inches simply to chop off the last paragraph of your piece – which can render the whole thing meaningless, or worse, turn its meaning upside down.

It does make you wonder, sometimes, why you bother (clue: the money), but it is essential that you learn to ignore it, otherwise it can destroy both motivation and concentration. These days, I almost never read anything of mine after it appears in print, because I just don't want to know (the exceptions, obviously, being facts – phone numbers and so on – which might need correcting. Like, I might need to send a note to an author saying 'I do apologise that the title of your fascinating book *My Life in Films* is printed here as *My Wife's a Flan*').

Don't let it get to you, then. But at the same time, if you ever have a chance to list a few of the subbing outrages which still rankle – in a book about freelancing, for instance – then grab it. Be cunning, though, be subtle: disguise your revenge as a list of tips.

1. Always assume that subs have no general knowledge. I recently wrote a piece about sports sponsorship for a political weekly, which ended with an admittedly feeble darts joke. After summarising my argument in three discrete points, I taunted the government with scoring a negative 'three in a bed'. The subs, who tend to work according to inflexible rules of good style, removed the '1, 2, 3' – but left the three in a bed gag hanging there at the end, like a blob of jam on a blanket.

My fault. I should not have taken it for granted that people who work on political weeklies watch sport on TV.

2. Always assume that subs will misunderstand you on every possible occasion. In a review of a collection of slipstream short stories, I compared the author to Kornbluth and Salinger. I meant C.M. Kornbluth and J.D. Salinger; indeed, having never heard of any other Kornbluthen or Salingerii, I didn't think it necessary to give them their initials. The subs, clearly being better read than me, and concerned that my ignorance might lead to confusion, spelled it out: Joseph Kornbluth and Pierre Salinger.

Did anybody notice? Did the author I was attempting to praise go mad trying to figure out what she had in common with Joe and Pete? I don't suppose so. But me, I still blush whenever I think of it.

3. Don't think you can shift the blame. A sub-editor is the person who prepares your copy for print. You might be surprised how many intelligent readers don't know that. When a sub introduces an error into your article, anyone who notices will naturally presume that the error is yours, and some of them will write to you about it. 'Dear Sir, In claiming that Britain's Prime Minister during World War Two was the Rt. Hon Winston Crackhouse, you not only reveal yourself as a moronic product of the state socialist comprehensive un-education system, but also spit on the graves of the brave men who died for your freedom. You are a disgrace, and I hope your dog gets AIDS. Yours Sincerely, A Christian.'

More worrying are those who spot the mistake, but don't write in about it. Instead they open to a certain page in a special notebook they carry for that purpose, and add your name to a list headed SO-CALLED WRITERS WHO KNOW NOTHING ABOUT ANYTHING.

4. Keep the jokes simple; the sub with a sense of humour has yet to be born. In a newspaper think piece about being a non-driver I wrote 'I must be the only male over seventeen for miles around who doesn't spend his evenings and weekends cacophonously tinkering and tuning'. That appeared as 'I must be the only male for over seventeen miles around who doesn't . . .'

As it happens, that feature was later sold by the paper to a German educational publisher for use in a school text book. I was very glad of the extra money, and being able to add another country to my CV, but I sometimes feel sorry for the teacher in Germany unable to answer his pupils when they ask 'Vot is ze zignificance of zeventeen miles, Herr Doktor? It zeems a strangely specific number, nein?'

5. Don't rise to it. Try not to respond to subbing cockups, except to correct serious factual errors. I say 'try', because I know it's not easy. I have long believed that some magazines employ dyslexic subs as part of a caring scheme. I am not alone in this (frankly barking) suspicion. There's a story (isn't there always? Yes, there is) about a writer who, maddened beyond circumspection by an unusually garbled article, faxed this message to his editor: 'If I promise to have sex with you, could my next column please be subbed by a sighted person?' The editor's reply was a small masterpiece of sadism: 'We do indeed have a progressive proprietor who employs a number of partially sighted subs, but your preferences have been noted'.

6. Eliminate surprise from your repertoire of reactions where subs are concerned. I once saw a three page feature in a glossy magazine in which the word 'while' was spelt 'wile' throughout. Now, there are only two things that could have happened here; either the writer spelt it wrongly, and the sub didn't notice; or else, and I think this is more likely, the author spelt it correctly, and the sub deliberately changed it because she thought it was wrong. Subs as a species are not only staggeringly ignorant but also fantastically arrogant. (Though not always; I received a very nice letter of apology from the *New Statesman* after the first instalment of a long-running column I wrote for them had included the rather bizarre suggestion that I had been educated at the nation's expense in a French brothel – as opposed to what I had written, which was that I *should* have been so educated.)

MORON SUBS   (Sorry: that should be 'more on subs'.)

Humorists undoubtedly suffer from subbing more than any other category of writer or journalist. Apart from the deadening effect of corrections and house style (subs, male or female, are like those girls at school who get A grades in English exams, even though they've never had an original thought, or read a book for pleasure), and the fact that subs don't get jokes for the same reason they don't get VD – they take precautions – a sub occasionally gets above himself, and sets out to improve the writer's gags.

I once worked to a sub who developed a comic fixation with the word 'katabatic'. Katabatic is a meteorological term, and thus of limited application, but I don't think he knew what it meant, or cared; he felt it possessed 'comedy consonants' and could therefore be used at will to liven up my duller passages. Mostly he achieved this by shoehorning it in as an irrelevant alliterative adjective (even though subs usually abhor the animated alliterative allusions which are one of the cheap tricks of the humorist's rough trade). For the duration of his obsession, I had to avoid using words which began with the 'k' sound; canine was out, feline was in.

Subs on highbrow titles religiously excise any phrase which sounds at all lively or interesting (whilst wearing indulgent smiles, I imagine). Subs on lowbrow magazines will go through your copy carefully reinstating every single cliché which you have spent hours trying to write your way around. In both cases, this is done for a reason. Highbrow periodicals are read by unintelligent, overeducated people who believe that anything which reads fluently is unworthy of their immensely valuable time, whereas lowbrow periodicals are staffed by grunting monkeys who can scarcely read or write, and who tend to believe that clichés hold some kind of semi-official status – that they are the only permitted or perhaps possible ways of saying something – and that you'll get into trouble if you don't use them.

Decent writers irritate them mightily, by creating extra work for them: 'For fuck's sake, this idiot's written "is being considered by the government". Now I've got to cross that out and put in "is being taken on board at this moment in time by the powers that be". As if I didn't have enough to do!'

It certainly doesn't occur to them that you might have omitted a cliché deliberately. Even if it did, they have such a low opinion of the readers (this is especially true of the staff on magazines with a mainly female readership) that their attitude is 'Better write it in language the poor bloody punters can cope with'.

I say again, don't let it get to you. Don't worry about what subs do to your words. Because the fact is, what you write isn't important. Nobody gives a toss but you. Nobody cares. You've written a piece explaining why you'd rather die than vote Tory, and the subs keep taking out the word not, and print the article under the headline WHY YOU MUST VOTE TORY by Lance Free. It doesn't matter. You wait for all your friends to ring you in an angry chorus, and gradually, when the phone doesn't ring, you begin to realise that nobody's read it. Or they've read it but didn't notice what it said. Or if they did notice what it said, they didn't care – they've got other things to think about. Relax. None of it matters. It drives you insane, yes, but it doesn't actually matter.

The title of the previous section was not randomly chosen. Spelling a contributor's name is, in fact, one of the many tasks that often seems too difficult for subs to manage. I am frequently by-lined as 'Matt', and more than once as 'Matt Howard'. One magazine made me 'Matt' on the by-line, and 'Nat' on the cheque.

Does it matter? Well, yes, a little. For the beginner, there is the famous 'thrill of seeing your name in print' – significantly diminished if it's not actually your name that's printed – and for all writers, the by-line is an important advertising medium.

I have had people to say to me, in all seriousness, 'I saw a good piece by a Matt Coward the other day. Do you ever get his cheques by mistake?' I have nightmares about Hollywood talent scouts searching through the Writers' Guild membership list for Matt ('Get me this Nat Howard guy! He's a genius!'), and giving up and going home when all they can find is Mat.

Besides, I suspect that half the time Matt is deliberately given the credit that should be mine. A streak of contemptuousness is a necessary quality for anyone who makes a living messing around with other people's copy, and I'm sure that some subs honestly believe I don't know how to spell my own name. 'Oh look – he's gone and typed it with only one T! He'll be glad I spotted that.' How does someone get to be that cocksure? I mean, of all the words on the page, is it really feasible that *that's* the one I'll have forgotten to check?

You'd think Coward would be a fairly memorable name, difficult to misspell. But even that gets helpfully corrected occasionally. I think subs feel sorry for me – 'Oh dear, he won't want people thinking his name's Coward. It's probably Howard, I'll change it for him.'

On the other hand, some employers go to extraordinary lengths to ensure accuracy. I made my TV debut on a satellite show (a deeply forgettable performance on a programme which was subsequently cancelled, for a company which no longer exists), and during the preceding week no less than eight individuals from the production office rang me to confirm my forename's T-count. You have to admire that kind of dedicated thoroughness; particularly so since the broadcast was a dummy run, and therefore the only people exposed to my on-screen caption were the few who were privileged to be in the studio that historic night.

By the way, if the name on the cover of this book is spelt wrongly (it should read 'Mac Howard'), you'll know that, as usual, a sub-editor has had the last laugh. Indeed, if he's done his job properly, it should be the only laugh in the book.

From subs to censorship, a natural progression. And let me say at the start that I am entirely in favour of censorship. I am especially in favour of censorship when it is applied to me.

A good sub-editor, and I have encountered one or two, exists to save the writer from himself; not only to render his prose comprehensible, but also to prevent him libelling the rich and powerful, to spot his errors of fact, and to make him think again about the lapses from good taste to which even the most courtly of us are occasionally prone. All of these necessary favours, subs have performed for me.

But that's enough balance.

The trouble with censorship is, they usually cut the wrong bit (admiring references to Joseph Stalin's treatment of religious dissidents, for instance, are almost always removed). And they are so bloody random in their likes and dislikes. The *New Statesman* wouldn't let me call Charles Fort the most important philosopher of the twentieth century, but did print my description of a female cabinet minister as 'looking like a toilet that someone had been sick into'.

The first time I ever wrote for the *New Statesman* (a humour piece, this was) I was phoned by a sub there who politely asked if I would mind her 'feminising 50% of my pronouns' (I told her I didn't mind what he did).

Sometimes you rely on the subs to censor you, so that you can let off steam by saying dreadfully obscene things about a public figure without getting into trouble for it, and they let you down. Years ago I wrote something absolutely horrific about the then Foreign Secretary, certain that it wouldn't get past the subs, and it did. Ever since, I've lived in fear of him buying a bag of chips wrapped in the offending article, and contacting a solicitor.

Or if not him, then any one of the dozen or so individuals, groups, nations and species also libelled in the course of the rather convoluted simile which comprised the insult.

If you don't want to be censored, write only for non-censoring markets. I don't remember ever being censored by a British small press magazine. The situation in the USA is more complicated.

American writing markets divide into two camps. First there are the crazy libertarians, who are only likely to suppress any paragraph which doesn't offend at least four major ethnic groups, two world religions and 17% of all known housewives. These are people who aren't aware that the US Constitution was written for a bit of a laugh by a bunch of bored students on a rainy Sunday afternoon in Wales when the pubs were closed in 1961. It was a hoax, the *Fortean Times* exposed it years ago, but these guys don't realise that, they think freedom of speech is actually supposed to mean something.

You won't get censored by them, but if you write for them you might get extradited to Alabama and jailed for life.

On the other hand, there are the descendants of the Puritans; people who think that the original Puritans probably meant well, but had a regrettable tendency to engage in far too much sex, laughter and public displays of emotion. These are the kind of editors who issue writers' guidelines saying (and this is an actual verbatim quote from an actual set of guidelines I actually received from an American SF mag a couple of years ago): 'Violence, explicit sex, and language are discouraged, as the editor feels a good story shouldn't rely on these elements'.

I didn't bother submitting a story to this po-faced editor. Even if I could have figured out how to write something without using language, I would have been too revolted by that horrible, sticky, suffocating schoolroom cliché about 'a good story' not needing sex, violence or swearing. (Or politics, I'll bet, or smoking, or unpleasant characters, or disrespect towards teddy bears, or . . . well, *language*, basically.)

'People only swear because they haven't got a big enough vocabulary to express themselves properly' – that's what they used to tell us at school. It was a load of arse then, and it's a load of arse now. I swear as much as possible (and only partly to distract attention from the titchiness of my vocab).

This comes from a British magazine, I'm ashamed to say: 'Anything very explicit should be avoided'. So remember to keep your images fuzzy, your metaphors imprecise, your politics post-modern, and your descriptions soft-focus: 'He was a medium sized man or woman with a beard or hat, and he came through the door carrying something or other in one of his hands'.

You wonder why these people are involved in publishing at all, when they are so clearly logophobic and have such a hatred of human expression. Obviously, you don't write for such people unless you really need the work, and meanwhile just pray you never come up against them in the Supreme Court in the case of State of Alabama vs *Stick It In Yer Ass* magazine. That's when you'll find out that their idea of 'profanity' is (I'm not joking here) the word 'damn', and that their idea of explicit sex is any mention of an ankle (I *am* joking there).

And there, my friends, is the entire history of the United States of America in a capsule.

When you're writing for mainstream markets, for magazines, TV, radio and so on, you'll just have to learn to live with censorship. Thing to remember is, it doesn't matter. It's just writing, it's not anything important, so don't get in a state about it.

I am constantly re-amazed at what I am and am not allowed to say by various editors. At the *New Statesman*, I was never allowed to call a woman a slag or a bitch – even if that woman was by her own admission a Liberal Democrat. When I wrote the word 'bitch' (as I did every bloody week, you can bloody depend on that, pal) the subs would replace it with 'woman'. Which makes you think, doesn't it? Are those two terms really interchangeable? Not to me they're not, but then I use the swollen vocabulary of a swearer, and thus perhaps have more words at my disposal. When I wrote of an adulterous MP and his 'tart', it was subbed to 'other woman'. I was allowed to call men anything I wanted, obviously. One week I wrote a whole piece about how to hunt, kill and eat Norwegians (they were increasing their whaling activities at the time). This was, necessarily, a gruesome piece, but only one part was cut. 'True gourmets', the unacceptable lines read, 'insist on female flesh, not more than four years old. After the age of about nineteen, Norwegian bitches become sinewy and bearded'.

Hey, so much for satire.

The same mag prevented me from calling Germaine Greer a 'prune-faced old nutter', which I thought was almost affectionate, all things considered. Besides, you can hardly imagine an intellectual colossus of Ms Greer's stature suing because someone she's never heard of denigrates her skin care regime, can you?

Another magazine I wrote for, one with a 'young independent woman' readership profile, changed my 'railway signalman' to 'railway signalperson', though I suppose it's just about possible that that one was a joke. It's so hard to tell these days.

One bit of censorship along these lines that I've heard of, but have never yet managed to achieve, is the now legendary 'Men who died fighting in the British Army against Hitler's troops' being amended to 'Men and women who died fighting in the British Army against Hitler's troops'. And of course we've all heard of the American newscaster who referred to Nelson Mandela as 'an African-American', because she knew she wasn't allowed to call him black and because, like all Americans, she had no idea that there existed a place in time-space which was Not-America. She hadn't even heard the rumours.

I noticed a couple of years ago that the *Daily Telegraph* allowed its then columnist, the former comedian Harry Enfield, to use the word 'arse', whereas elsewhere in the paper this medical term was spelled 'a**e', and who you are certainly determines to some extent how much censorship you can expect to encounter. I can't imagine the *Daily Mail*, for instance, ringing up George Bush and complaining that 'You've described Colin Powell as an African-American. We usually prefer the term "black bastard", would that be all right?'.

Almost all routine censorship is unnecessary (even by the standards of the censors, I mean) and done out of either fear or stupidity or both. Stephen Fry told a funny story in an interview a few years ago, about the column he was then writing for the *Telegraph*. One week he complained, in his characteristically ironic style, of the BBC's 'frankly Marxist coverage of Wimbledon'. This was changed to 'politically biased coverage of Wimbledon', which suggests, as Fry noted, that 'they genuinely think the tennis coverage is Marxist'.

The trouble with good subs (as distinct from the stupid ones) is that they are rational and level-headed. They need to be sent on a day release course in hyperbole. In my time as a controversialist, I was forever finding soppy little words like 'indeed' or phrases like 'it might be argued' inserted into my copy, or inverted commas placed around certain words to defuse them, in order to make me sound slightly less mad than I in fact am. I think this is unfair on the reader. If a columnist happens to be completely bonkers, it is really no job of the editorial staff to protect readers from this distressing information. To give the reader the impression that he is reading the words of a sane man is *it could be argued* the most dangerous of all forms of censorship.

. . . is the simple and final answer to that question so beloved of contributors to writers' mags who think they're writers because they've had four letters in a row accepted by *Fat Cow* magazine – namely, 'Should I get an agent?'.

Many writers, both the agented and the unagented, will tell you that it is easier to find a publisher to buy your book than it is to find an agent to sell your book. They're not joking: one function of the agent system is to act as a preliminary filter – to prevent the slushiest slush ever getting within slopping distance of the publishers' slush piles.

There are some agents, and some agencies, who actively seek fresh, young talent. But, hey, what they do in their spare time is their own business, right? There are also some who are genuinely interested (as opposed to slogan-parrotingly interested) in working with new writers. The best way of finding out which ones these are at any particular time (because agents, like editors, move around a lot, possibly for reasons of personal security), is to ask writers with whom you're acquainted whether they're represented, and if so is their agent any good. If that fails, ask writers with whom you're not acquainted: 'Dear Author, I am a big fan of your work. I'm also a writer, and have had a number of articles and short stories published (none of which I am enclosing with this letter, because I'm not some nutty fanboy pest with no manners). I feel that at this stage in my career I need an agent to guide me, and wonder if you would be kind enough to let me know who represents you? Obviously, I am not asking for an introduction, merely for a name and address which I can use as a starting point. I enclose a SAE for your convenience (because an SAE is what every convenience needs, right?) and grovel grovel thanks thanks grovel your last book is easily your best yet etc'. Send it c/o his publishers, and I'd be surprised if, of the ten writers you wrote this letter to, at least two didn't reply with helpful advice.

And if all else fails, put together a portfolio and a CV and simply send it to every agent listed in the appropriate reference books in your local library. You never know, maybe one of them will bother to reply sometime in the following eighteen months. But don't hold your breath.

Or you could do what I did, which is get an agent completely by accident and without lifting a finger. Unfortunately, for this to work you would need to have spent quite a lot of time in the early to mid 1980s drinking (and, latterly, playing quiz machines) in pubs in the Waterloo area of London, so possibly my mentioning this is not particularly helpful and could even be filed under the 'Smug Bastard Asking for a Kicking' heading. Sorry.

For most forms of freelancing, an agent is unnecessary. They are usually only interested in, and useful for, the big ticket items; chiefly books. Many publishers say up-front that they don't look at unagented manuscripts. Some publishers don't say it up front, but it's true nonetheless. Even those who say they're happy to look at unagented submissions, will generally admit that they rarely buy anything from that corner of their desks.

If you've got something specific to sell – I mean, the typescript of your book is right there, ready to roll – then send it round the agents before you send it round the publishers. (Some agents, like some publishers, prefer preliminary letters. The reference books will tell you which ones. You can read, can you?)

The new, smaller publishers tend not to be so bothered about the agented/unagented hierarchy. As it may well be that such houses are the future of publishing, while the big old firms die off, then it may well be that not being agented is going to become less of a problem. There again, as the small firms thrive, they will grow; as they grow, they will begin to receive thousands of MSS a week instead of hundreds; and eventually they will have to institute some version of an 'agents only' rule, because otherwise they will never get to read anything worth publishing.

Apart from the respectability which an agent's endorsement attaches to your MS, there are two other less obvious advantages to having decent representation. I discovered them when I was trying to sell a children's novel. My then agent took it on, and sent it round to the six leading children's editors. None of them bought the book, and they all replied at some length saying why they didn't.

If I had been trying to sell the book myself, as I know from tedious experience, first of all I wouldn't have dared send it out to six publishers simultaneously; simultaneous submission is, in the writing manuals, the kind of terrible *faux pas* that premature ejaculation is in the sex manuals. But agents can get away with that kind of kinky stuff. I would have had to wait months for the first one to reject it, then print out a new copy because you never send an old, tatty copy of anything to anyone, and take it down to the post office to send it off to the next editor on the list, and so on for the next year or so of my life. I'd have been paying the not inconsiderable postage and photocopying charges, instead of the agent paying them, and at the end of it I wouldn't have got detailed and potentially useful rejection letters – I'd have got a printed slip wishing me luck in placing it elsewhere.

They have their uses, you see, agents do – even when they're not selling anything for you.

HOW TO GET A BOOK PUBLISHED (FORGET IT)

You might as well forget it, you know. You are never going to get your book published (even if you ever manage to finish one, ha ha ha). I mean it: the odds against are fantastic.

For a start, if you haven't got an agent you can double forget it. Yes, yes, I know, I've seen the stories in the papers too: 'Forecourt attendant lands million dollar deal with crayon manuscript. "I wrote it on bog paper to impress my cat," says record-breaking first-time author'.

But consider this: 'Man farts in bath' never appears on the front page of a newspaper because it is not a sufficiently uncommon occurrence. 'Unagented book sells' is, and that's why it is on the front page. Most publishers won't even look at unagented manuscripts. They haven't got time. They haven't got the staff (they've downsized their staffage in order to increase efficiency, which is why they haven't got time to do half the work they used to do when they were inefficiently overstaffed. No, I'm not obsessed with this, I'm just right).

Those publishers who do look at unagented MSS don't buy any of them, or at least not more often than a country you've never heard of wins the World Cup. It happens, it happens, I know it happens – but it's not going to happen to you. It just isn't. (I suppose I ought to mention here that, as it happens, I have sold all but one of my books unagented; however, I did so more through luck than judgement and, as a result, spend more time reading contracts than I do sleeping.)

Of course some people have wonderful relationships with their publishers and go on to be happy with them and to make a good living with them for years on end. But then there's everybody else.

And what everybody else says about publishers is that they're not interested in hearing from you. That if they do hear from you they're unlikely to reply. That if they do feel obliged to reply it'll only be with a form letter. That if they can't avoid considering your book they'll take at least a year to say 'No'. That if they can't find any way of not saying 'Yes', then they'll take another year to get the book published. And that once the book is published they will feel justified in considering the entire distasteful matter closed and you will never hear from them again after publication day.

Publishing it has to be said is not an industry largely populated by creative geniuses. Clever charismatic capable young people do not turn to each other in their last year at university and exclaim 'I'm not going to waste my life in some dead end job! I want to make a real difference in this world! I want to write my name in the stars! Hey guys – *I'm going into publishing!*'.

Publishing tends to be inhabited by rather listless girls who carry the kind of forenames which only the upper classes (or Australians) would not be embarrassed to give to their children; and by dreary men who are far more interested in wine and foreign travel than they are in books and writers.

Old-timers tell us of the days when publishers were gentlemen, which I take to mean that they knew nothing about selling books, even though they knew a fair bit about books. Today's publishers, the last generation in a dying industry, are super duper whizz kid computer programming accountants, which means that they don't know how to sell books either, for the scientific reason that they are all a load of wankbuckets.

Publishers are thick. If you write a book that has a child protagonist – or even worse, a child narrator – then make sure you have the word 'fellatio' somewhere on the first page, otherwise, no matter what the style, content or subject matter, an editor will simply scan the first few lines, realise the book is about children, conclude therefore that it's *for* children, and send it back with a note saying 'We don't do children's fiction'. No, honestly, that's how simple these people are.

Publishing is basically a career for upper-class women who were too ugly and disagreeable to get married straight from finishing school.

My first book was published by a major publisher, and despite all the cheap jokes above I have to say that all the people I dealt with there were quite charming. They did a nice job on the book too; attractive cover, great illustrations. They didn't manage to sell any, but that's not really their fault – it was a humour book, and all humour books (and there are a lot of them) are published at the same time, for the Christmas market. To win shelf space, your humour book really needs to be written, or at least to appear under the name of, a TV celebrity, and mine didn't.

So the charming publishers took a gamble on my book, it didn't come off, never mind.

The best laugh I had during the whole process was when I saw my entry in the publisher's forthcoming attractions list. It read: 'Mat Coward reviews for the *Evening Standard* [I never have], the *Guardian* [I never have], the *Independent* [I hadn't then but I have since – spooky!] and the *Observer* [I never have]. He features regularly on Radio 4's *Loose Ends* [I had, but eight years earlier] and *Pick of the Week* [there are no regulars on *PotW*, as its name rather implies]. He lives in London [I did; that was the only fact they got right]'.

I, like more and more writers, including many long-established and still successful novelists, feel increasingly that the future lies with the 'Big Small Press': those small, independent, ambitious, rock-hard, often one-man publishing outfits who have achieved sufficient velocity to escape the orbit of the planet Doomed-By-The-Third-Issue-Fanzine, but have not disappeared into the black hole of mainstream moribundity. (Apologies to any astrophysicists reading; I get all this from comics you know, I don't make any claims for its veracity.)

For economic reasons, and others, the best of these Big Smalls have a flexibility, an ability to survive crises, an appetite for the job, and an openness to new ideas and writers, that would be unimaginable in the spiralling-to-its-doom world of mega-merger publishing houses in these last days (I says, Last Days) of late-period capitalism. They are battle-hardened, which means that they've already got about as weary, wounded and broke as they're ever likely to get. If you ever see a small press publisher walking funny, it's because he's sold his rectum for medical research to raise money to buy a colour printer. The Big Smalls are Darwinism in action: they've survived the worst that can be fired at them by an economic system specifically designed to drive them out of business, and they've evolved specialist new genes to deal with it all.

Or at least, they might read your manuscript, which is more than can be said for the megas.

The fact that you're reading this book means that you have already discovered the existence of the Big Smalls; follow up on that discovery methodically and urgently, is my advice.

Monopolisation of the book trade and the decrease in library book funds have led to fiction publishing becoming a vanishing circle: even if you could get your book published, there'll be no budget for promotion, it'll effectively go out of print about a week after it's published, there are no backlists any more.

As a book reviewer, I see a lot of publishers' press releases, and I can tell you that it is very unusual to come across a press release that is written in comprehensible English, that has been proofread, that doesn't spell the author's name wrong, or give the title of the book incorrectly, and doesn't contain at least one sentence that has no discernible meaning.

If you want your book publicised, you'd better do it yourself – and not merely by rearranging the displays in your local bookstores. Big publishers seem to issue their books under a D Notice, to prevent anyone finding out about them. All authors feel this way: I daresay even John Grisham thinks he's underpublicised. When he's Number One in every hardback, paperback and movie chart in the world, he probably still says to his wife 'Why don't those damn publishers just print the books in invisible ink and have done with it! Jeez, only 22 million copies sold since Tuesday – I might as well get a job pumping gas!'.

If logic counted for anything, half our GNP would be spent on public libraries. Free libraries are by far the cheapest, most efficient, most effective way of distributing knowledge (quite apart from their literally irreplaceable role in distributing entertainment); this is more true than ever, since the invention of the internet and related technologies. Every public penny invested in public libraries is recouped by the public purse a thousandfold, through the taxation paid in later life by library-inspired writers, inventors and entrepreneurs.

Libraries, along with public services generally, have fallen victim to the insane idea that public spending is in some way a bad thing; the desperate, nationally suicidal obsession with 'saving' money, as if a nation's treasury were a one parent family living on inadequate benefits; the mad belief that a nation cannot profit from anything that is not profitable.

These forms of lunacy which have become so familiar and so fashionable in the last two decades are being used to attack the single best idea anyone ever had; there's no way of making a profit out of a public library service and so, according to the perverted logic of the ranting right, this proves that there's no demand for it.

But we should not be surprised that, now when they are at their most valuable, libraries are being systematically destroyed. Sections of the ruling class always opposed their existence; specifically, their principle of universality, which, once widely accepted, means the inevitable death of class society. Libraries cause civilisation to happen. They are, at least as much as the secret ballot, a keystone of democracy. Public libraries allow the landless to *own* knowledge.

They also, less controversially, allow writers to feed their children. Or they used to, before 1979 and the Plague of the Evil One (you think evil is too strong a word? Remember, the same monster was in power when *Dr Who* was cancelled).

In 1997 a report by the Audit Commission said that in the past decade, book issues nationally had fallen by 19% – that's 108 million issues. However, libraries were still by far the most popular of all public services, 24 million adults in England and Wales being members of their library, and 460 million issues taking place per year. The library service cost the equivalent of £13 per head of the population per year. Library spending on books in the decade up to 1997 fell by 10%, even though libraries accounted for just one per cent of local authority expenditure.

Opening hours have been cut massively, as the insane dictum 'reduce staffing at any cost' became the only governing principle in public and private initiative, throughout the western world. Libraries do seem to be increasingly popular with children, which is a hopeful sign, but the bad news is that the decline in book issues has occurred mainly in the field of adult popular fiction. So this might be a good time to switch from SF sagas to baby books.

Also in 1997, HarperCollins, Rupert Murdoch's gigantic publishing company, announced in New York that it was cutting over one hundred books from its list having made a $7m operating loss in the first three months of the calendar year. A spokesman sent this message to would-be writers: 'Please don't bother sending us your manuscripts, because we couldn't afford to publish them even if we wanted to, which, believe me, we don't'. Well, she didn't, actually, but she might as well have done.

As well as the effects of 'economic realism' (ie underinvestment and short-termism and asset-stripping) on public library budgets, publishers have also suffered from their own stupidity, contempt for their customers and lack of knowledge of the book trade. In the late 1980s and early 90s, hundreds of millions of pounds were paid in advances to celebrity authors for their self-glorifying drivel. (The usual assumption is that celebooks are ghostwritten, but that misses the point; ghostwritten means written by a professional writer. If they had been ghostwritten they wouldn't have been such drivel.)

As could have been predicted by anyone with any intelligence at all – that is, almost anyone who doesn't work in publishing – these books only rarely earned back the author's advances, let alone the enormous publicity budgets. For years, the publishing industry has wasted its time trying to sell books to people who don't buy books, while neglecting to take care of its existing assets, its writers and readers. The result is, *bleeding obviously*, that people who don't buy books continue not to buy books, while those who would like to buy books can't, because they are being asked to subsidise the talk show host's three million quid advance, and those who would like to write the books that customers might buy a year or ten years from now are unlikely to do so because they can't make anything approaching a living at it. And all this came as a great surprise to the publishing industry.

Idiot stupid bastard fools. Hang everyone in the world who earns more than fifty grand a year, and all the world's problems will disappear overnight. I guarantee it.

FRENCH MUSTARD IS FOR GIRLS!

I saw an ad for a daily broadsheet recently which described a pair of the paper's columnists as 'two of Britain's leading controversialists'. For some reason, that really cracked me up. The idea of there being *two* of them: did they have adjacent desks? Would they spend all their time disagreeing with each other? 'Look, for the *last* sodding time, single-sex grammar schools are the future of education in the twenty-first century and that is *my* coffee mug and you are forbidden to use it!'

They'd *have* to disagree with each other, wouldn't they? Otherwise they wouldn't be controversialists. They'd be consensusists.

'Smoking should be banned, you know.'

'Ah yes, but on the other hand old chap, there should be a ban on smoking.'

In any case, being even *one* of Britain's leading controversialists – isn't that rather a contradiction in terms? Surely the whole point of being a controversialist is being an outsider, an enemy of the state, a fearless dissident – not someone who is by common consent jolly good at disagreeing; someone so harmless that an organ of the establishment can trumpet you as 'leading'.

Writers can be controversial, but to be a specialist in controversy – it's all a bit cold and clinical isn't it? A bit controlled, a bit regulated. Allowed. Permitted. Fake. You can imagine them going to a Controversy Academy. Or perhaps they studied it at Cambridge; while their friends were doing Politics, Philosophy & Economics, they were doing CCC – Contrariness, Colourfulness & Cuteness.

And they probably have dozens of annual meaningless award ceremonies, like the advertising industry. Best Use of Bile In An Eight Hundred Word Think Piece Attacking British Muslims For Not Fitting In And Wondering How They'd Like It If We Behaved Like That In Their Bloody Country Eh?

These tame controversialists, with their haw-haw laughs and their florid faces and their big houses – they think they're devil's advocates, but really they're only weevil's advocates.

And the runner-up in Using The Phrase Political Correctness Ten Times In One Paragraph goes to . . .

Could have been me, truth is. Bit close to the bone, all this stuff. See, I was a professional controversialist for several years. I got out from under eventually, but I still have the occasional moment when I'm standing in a pub having a quiet drink and I suddenly hear myself say 'You know, everyone thinks the nuclear holocaust is a bad idea, but that's only because they haven't bothered to think it through properly'.

Editors think they love controversy. They use letters of outrage as an index of success. I find this approach rather smug. It reminds me of the way that whenever the BBC's accused of bias its spokesmen always say 'Well, you know, we're accused of bias by both the left and the right, so that means we must be getting it about right, doesn't it?'. No, fool, it just means that you're biased towards the centre – which, in a democracy, is the most damaging bias of all.

The idea is that intelligent people enjoy reading strongly expressed opinions with which they disagree. It's not true. Nobody likes being confronted with contradictory opinions. You'd have to be mad to enjoy that. How controversy columns work, to the extent that they work at all, is by giving pleasure to those who agree with them, but who don't dare speak their thoughts so stridently, or write them so eloquently.

Shortly after John Major became prime minister I was hired to write a weekly controversy column for a liberal political magazine. My brief, as far as I can remember, was along the lines of 'Be controversial. Generate a lot of mail'. I wasn't that keen on the job, but regular work is regular work (ie hell on earth but irresistible), so I wrote a piece outlining my opposition to education in all its forms, and I was away.

I certainly generated lots of mail. Much of it was hate mail, but a significant proportion was from readers who evidently took great comfort from reading views which chimed with their own, and which were not widely available in the mainstream media. I began the column with a kind of persona in mind – as I was writing humorous pieces from the point of view of an old-fashioned, anti-fashionable, anti-liberal socialist, I thought of myself as Coco the Stalinist – but after a while this became too tiresome to maintain, and I ended up writing as myself.

There are many unpleasant jobs available to the freelance writer, but that of house controversialist is one of the worst. If you're doing the thing properly, you need to develop a thin skin, to suffer a degree of personal exposure which most sane people would find uncomfortable. Writing with honesty is hard work. It makes your brain bleed.

There's a law of diminishing returns in the controversy game. If you start your new column in the first week with 'All human beings should be killed in death camps' you can't really follow up in week two with 'Liquorice isn't all it's cracked up to be'.

I knew it had all gone too far the day I was invited to become a radio shock jock. I don't know if you've ever heard any of these morons. I haven't, as it happens, but I still have strong opinions on them ('They should be forced to eat their own children' – read Britain's leading controversialist only in tomorrow's *Daily Doily*. He's shocking, he's outspoken, he tells it like it is! He's a 42-year-old middle-class dad living in an over-mortgaged link-detached 3-bedroom house in Hatch End!).

I'd had enough of being controversial. No one takes you seriously when you are being serious, because they know that you get paid for being controversial. Being truthful every week and being controversial are not always compatible.

Not all conts (no seriously, that's the recognised standard abbreviation) even try to be honest. The real tragedy of the kept controversialist is not that he has too many opinions, or daft opinions, or offensive opinions, but that he has no real opinions at all. There's one leading controversialist on a tabloid national who keeps writing the same piece over and over again. Of course, we all do that to some extent, but this bloke *really* does it. The same items, the same jokes, often in precisely the same words. Once he wrote an entire page made up of what he presumably thought were some of his greatest hits – but he presented it as if it was all new. At that level, it can't be just forgetfulness or idleness, it must be deliberate piss-taking (or irony, as the studenty types call it).

You can often witness a domino effect amongst the nation's professional conts, when one after another of them adopts a new official idea. Perhaps you remember the classic 'If global warming's true, then how come it's so cold this summer?'. Or fox-hunting; that was a perfect example. Throughout the summer of 1997, when a private member's bill to abolish field sports was going through the House of Commons, every single London-based broadsheet columnist suddenly came out in favour of the hunt. Not one of them had ever seen a hunt, not one of them knew anything about the subject, they were simply trying to be different. Which is why, within about a fortnight, every last one of them was singing the same, 'controversial' song.

These are not people of great imaginative skills.

(Oh yes they are! Oh no they're not!)

4: Bad advice and where to find it

AN EXPERT WRITES   I've just seen an advertisement in a newspaper headed 'How to make money writing short paragraphs'.

Can I have my money now, please?

Not that the paragraphs in the ad itself (for a £15 book) are actually all that short; even so, I think the first par is worth reprinting in full: 'Here is a little-known angle by which beginners often get paid five to ten times more per word than the rates paid to famous authors. Now anyone who can write a sentence in plain English can write for money without sacrificing time and money learning how to write'.

In fact, that's not my favourite ever writing advertisement. *This* is my favourite ever, from an invitation to subscribe to a correspondence course: 'Every year about two thousand novice writers become successful authors. They see their names on a published children's book for the first time. Yet they are no different from you. They have no special talent, no natural gift, no literary flair'.

Wow: no talent, no gift, no flair – just like me! Makes you wonder why we haven't *all* 'seen our names on a published children's book for the first time', doesn't it? Even more, it makes you wonder how people who have written children's books have got the sheer bloody cheek to hold their heads up in public, given that what they do requires no special talent, no natural gift, and no literary flair.

Scrounging, giftless bastards! Never mind seeing their names on published children's books, they should be bloody *prosecuted*, that's what they should be, bloody prosecuted for bloody fraud. Bloody con merchants, all two thousand of them.

Because writing's easy, so it is; dead easy. Peasy-weasy. And making £££ from writing is even peasier.

I've got proof. This is another correspondence course come-on: 'A recent survey shows that freelance writers can earn very good money in their spare time writing the stories, articles, books, scripts etc that editors and publishers want. Millions of pounds are paid annually in fees and royalties. Earning YOUR share can be fun, profitable and creatively fulfilling'.

I must have missed that recent survey – probably because I haven't got any spare time, let alone enough of it to earn MY share of millions of pounds by servicing all those desperate, begging-for-it editors and publishers. I'm far too busy writing; writing, and *not* earning 'very good money'.

One of the 'distance learning schools' even offers a 24-hour Freephone number, in case you just can't wait to get started on your great new career. 'Freelance writing can be creative, fulfilling and a lot of fun', it says. 'With excellent money to be made as well. What's more, anyone can become a writer. No special qualifications or experience are required.'

Nonetheless, the same announcement insists that 'If you want to enjoy the rewards of seeing your work in print, one thing you *must* have is proper training'. Experience here on Planet Earth would seem to suggest that proper training is perhaps the least essential pre-requisite for a successful career in writing, but let's not quibble over details. However you get there, your journey to Writerland will certainly be worth it, because 'The market for writers is huge' and 'With such demand, there's always room for new writers'.

But let's just pop back to the first ad I quoted for a moment, because there's a line there that really caught my imagination; that bit about getting paid ten times more per word than famous authors. Right, now this is exactly the sort of upbeat, positive stuff beginners most need to hear, in my view: a valuable and much-needed antidote to all the pessimistic moaning full-time writers are always coming out with.

Take, for instance, famous author John Grisham. Admittedly, Grisham has earned hundreds of millions of pounds from a mere handful of novels; but (and this bit's important, right, this is the whole point) they are all fairly *long* books. So, when you work out your pay-per-word – your actual basic wordage, yeah? – it's not nearly as impressive as the initial raw data might suggest.

Compared to yourself, say, who's bought all these books and done all these courses and as a direct result succeeds in placing a humorous letter in a leading women's magazine, thus netting a cool five pounds for no more than, maybe, twenty or twenty-five words. Could be fifteen pounds, don't forget, if you're lucky enough to scoop the Star Letter. And all for – what? Ten minutes work? Literally. Now that, my friend, that is easy money by anybody's standards.

'£180 a day' is how much you can expect to earn from writing, provided 'you can write a letter', by following a 'formula' and learning certain 'simple secrets' which will be 'shared' with you in a 'new, comprehensive guide'.

The really important thing to bear in mind, and I make no apologies for repetition because this is vital information, is that there is no skill or talent or hard work involved in writing. None at all. The key point is that up until now 'a relatively few people have had a corner' on profitable markets. It is, in fact, as you always suspected it was, not what you do but what you know. It's a conspiracy, of course it is, and for just fifteen quid you can learn all the insider's secrets you'll ever need, to achieve a creatively fulfilling, high-paying, *fun* writing career.

From the same company that tells you how to make money writing short paragraphs comes this advice: 'If you want a firm, rounded, shapely bottom, you should know about a new book *Buttocks of Steel*. The book shows you a simple and fast way to give yourself neat, trim buttocks – even if other attempts to firm your bottom have failed'. And that's important, too, you know, because sitting down writing all day can play havoc with the condition of your buttocks. Believe me, I know, I have to really watch my bottom, day in day out. Even famous authors, you'll find, often employ people to watch their bottoms for them. (These people are called agents.)

However, I've got to say there is one ad I've seen in a writers' magazine which I feel I should warn you against, because it's obviously rubbish. 'Compliment your talent', it says, 'with software that really works'.

Well hell, I don't need some expensive software to help me compliment my talent! I do that every day, all on my own. Yes I do, I wake up every morning and the first thing I do is, I say: 'Yo, talent baby! You're looking especially creative, fulfilling and fun this fine morn, if one might make so bold!'.

And my talent giggles and bats its eyelids and goes all girlie, and then it pretends to get cross and speak very sternly (it's really quite sexy, I have to admit), and it says: 'Oh get on with you, you naughty man. You're only saying that because you want to *use* me!'.

Of all the depressing things you could do during your stay on our lovely homeworld of

Earthland plc, few would provide quite such an intensely saddening experience as a slow coach tour through the 'So You Wanna Be A Writer' Theme Park.

If, messieurs and mesdames, you belong to one of those higher races of ultra-evolved alien lifeforms which feed on human pain and indignity, then this is one attraction you can't afford to miss. All-inclusive admission price: £££.

A few years ago a book came out called *How To Write a Million*, the complete guide to becoming a successful author. Four hundred and ninety-four pages. I didn't buy a copy, and I was very glad I hadn't when, not long afterwards, a sequel appeared: *More About How To Write a Million, The Essential Guide to Becoming a Successful Author*. Five hundred and forty pages.

Boy oh boy, talk about yer actual bunch of suckers, eh? Ha ha! Imagine what a mug you'd feel if you'd bought a book that was a *complete guide* to its subject, only to find out that it's so damn *complete* that it needs a five hundred and forty page sequel!

The HowToWrite business – books, magazines, courses, services – is a sizeable industry (worth, indeed, £££); and, it has to be said, a slightly distasteful one. It is based on the premise that selling false hope has always be an easy way to make money. A famous con-man once said that if you want to make a million you should start your own church; well, servicing would-be writers may not be quite as tax efficient a way of conning the mugs, but it'll leave you pretty warm in a cold night, all the same.

Before I get too carried away with the stench of despair and dishonesty which inevitably lingers over this subject, I must give some prominence here to a sort of pre-emptive retraction: yes, HowToWrite books and mags can be useful.

For those of us who don't come to writing through the approved route (that is, university and family contacts), the HowTo books can be valuable in the very early stages of attempted freelancing. They can provide reassurance, a degree of inspiration, and even, very occasionally, the odd piece of useable information.

Even the magazines (the better produced ones that is; the others aren't worth glancing at) can come up with genuinely worthwhile market information. I once followed up a market info piece I read in a glossy monthly, and as a direct result landed a regular magazine column which, over a few years, earned me several thousand pounds. It probably goes without saying that I was the only 'writer' responding to that news item to whom the editor bothered replying; all the rest, as she put it, were 'embarrassing amateurs looking for a breakthrough'.

(This does seem to suggest that I was the only full-time writer desperate enough to follow up a market tip in a would-be-writers' mag, which certainly fits with what we know of my career profile.)

Ironically, although the magazines are read by would-be writers rather than by working writers, the market information they contain is potentially of value to freelances, while unlikely to be very helpful to the retired colonels and bored housewives and Christian poets who are actually reading it. It's a strange fact that there is no commercial magazine in this country for professional writers, only for would-be and hobbyist writers.

Borrow the HowToWrite books from the library, then, when you're starting out, and keep an eye on the market info pages of the magazines, but ignore the HowTo advice. Apart from anything, its often semiliterate and always cliché-soaked style (actual quote: 'With half the year well and truly over and the summer approaching its peak, July is the month for gearing ourselves towards success') will at best depress you and at worst might have an adverse influence on your own writing.

Remember: far more people make a living writing HowToWrites than make a living as a result of reading them.

And as for those heartbreaking 'Readers' Successes' columns – 'Belinda Hopeless has had letters accepted by *Knitwear Today*, the *Latex Trades Journal* and *Migraine News*. Well done, Belinda!' – reading them and weeping might be an appropriate response, but not reading them at all will be better for your health.

If you are tempted to send money in response to advertisements like 'Send us the first three chapters of your book for a statistical analysis of marketability' or 'Writers! Sell 90% of your finished output!' then I suspect you are beyond help. If you want to get your bottom firmed up by mail order, however, don't let me stop you. Hey, what do I know about firm bottoms?

'Write what you know' is invariably the advice given to new writers, and to an extent it's fair enough. But what if you don't know anything? Or what if what you do know is boring, or already known by everyone else? Or you're not sure what you do know, but suspect that if you did know, it might not be terribly exciting?

The answer then is to bluff a little.

For obvious reasons I can't give too many real-life examples of what I mean here, but there's one which shouldn't do too much harm to my credibility. In my late twenties I became extremely interested in vegetable gardening, and very quickly started selling a few garden advice articles to non-specialist publications – some to prestigious, well-paying markets.

I didn't exaggerate my expertise – that would have been risky, as well as unethical – but I did allow the editors to draw their own conclusions as to the extent of my authority. My covering letters didn't claim that I was a Visiting Professor of Onions at Oxbridge Horticultural College; on the other hand, the letters didn't read 'Dear Editor, I know nothing about gardening. Here is an article on gardening which I hope you can use'.

I bluffed a little, and counted on the fact that most editors would assume I knew what I was talking about, otherwise why would I be sending in the piece? I stuck to the crucial principle of not writing about anything I didn't know – a crop I'd never grown for instance – but I managed to imply in my tone of writing that I knew more than I was saying, and was choosing not to include it so as not to baffle the poor layman.

If I needed to provide a bit of information that wasn't strictly within my own knowledge, I would use a form of words such as 'It is often claimed in the literature that . . .' and then stick in a paraphrase cribbed from a gardening book. Yes, I wrote about what I knew, but I interpreted that injunction in as creative a way as I reasonably could. I made it an elastic boundary instead of a glass ceiling.

Looking back now at the stuff I wrote then, with the greater practical knowledge I've gained since, I find very little I'd need to change were I rewriting them today. I knew little about gardening, but I made very sure of my facts, and what little I did know I was perfectly capable of stretching out to whatever length an editor might want, and more than capable of making it read as if it had been written by an expert.

Proof that I got away with it (apart from the cheques) came with the readers' letters I received from fellow gardeners, many of which were addressed to 'Dr Coward'. The class system was definitely working in my favour here: educated people not only believe that none but the educated can write anything worth reading – they also believe that none but the educated would dare to try.

(Incidentally, I know someone who writes quite regularly about music, but who couldn't sing, play, whistle or hum a single note in tune if you put a gun to his head. Perhaps more surprisingly, he couldn't even if you *didn't* put a gun to his head.)

No, don't write what you know – I know it's what everybody tells you to do, but what do they know?

Instead, if you're going to write fiction, get yourself a genre.

If I have a theme as a book reviewer, by which I suppose I mean if there is one thing which I repeat *ad nauseum*, it is only this: the primacy of story. There should always be a story. It is the story – a chain of events leading to some sort of resolution – that turns a sketch into a novel. Good writing is always welcome, and new techniques and ideas can be exciting, but the story is the essential element; the rest is frills.

(There is, incidentally, nothing wrong with repeating yourself in print. There are three or four things I have to say to the world. They haven't changed much in the last decade or so, I don't expect they'll change much between now and my death, and I repeat them in every joke, story, radio talk or article that I write.)

Story is the difficult bit. I could write award-winning literary genius stuff twelve hours a day every day with my left hand whilst tossing off a donkey with my right hand. I really could. I could write that stuff jumping out of an aeroplane on my first ever parachute jump. I could write that stuff watching a stripper or opening the batting for England or during my spare time whilst earning my living as Chancellor of the Exchequer. I really could.

There is nothing easier in the world than writing litshit. The reason is that writing is merely a talent. (If you can do it you can do it. The problem is to get you to *stop* doing it.) Whereas storytelling is a skill or craft. Writing is something you're born with, like the ability to whistle in tune; if you've got a decent ear you can whistle in tune, but learning to play the guitar, you have to actually *do* that. It is something conscious.

Any genre will do, but crime fiction is favourite.

Cri-fi has been the saviour of so many writers who were talented, who knew they could write, be witty, come up with interesting characters, locations, smells and all that, but who, to their terrible frustration, just couldn't find anything to actually write about. All they could manage for years were half finished novels about all the wacky characters in the office or café or warehouse where they had their first job after leaving college. Like soup without bread: nothing to hold it all together, no plot.

Then one day, idly mooching around the library shelves, they chance upon a cri-fi novel which catches their eye for some reason (not the jacket design, that's for certain), and before they know what they're doing they're reading crime. Ah well, as long as nobody sees them it can't do much harm.

They'd given up cri-fi when they were thirteen years old, having exhausted Miss Christie's oeuvre, disdainfully banishing the entire genre as 'puzzle fiction'. True, at the age of eighteen or nineteen, there had been the brief, passionate, almost compulsory fling with Raymond Chandler – for the excellence of the writing and the wilful incomprehensibility of the plots. But Chandler, they were taught, 'transcended his genre', and thus they leave the crime shelves, never to return, except by fateful accident.

That accident having occurred, their eyes are suddenly opened. Modern crime fiction, they see, is somewhere where they could do everything they've ever wanted to do as a writer (characters, locations, style, experimentation, humour, moral struggle, philosophical speculation, sex scenes), and at the same time their books will have some kind of backbone, their soup will contain beans, *big beans*, their plots will have a kind of natural, inescapable shape.

From then on they never look back, and this is the reason (and this really is a trade secret) that there are many successful, critically acclaimed crime writers who never read crime fiction. It is not their natural habitat. They work there, but they don't want to live there. They commute.

FREE STUFF, SWEETER THAN WAGES

The worst advice I have ever received in my writing life was 'Ooh no you mustn't do that!'.

For several years around the time of Margaret Thatcher's second term I used to play petanque (which – and you might want to get your notebooks out here – is the most widely-played and competitively organised version of the game known generically as boules) a couple of times a week, on a purpose-built terrain, consisting of two pistes, which dear old Camden Council had caused to be laid in the foothills of Primrose Hill in north London.

Directly across the road from the Snowdon Birdcage, in fact. If you'd walked along that road one evening in midsummer with your eyes closed, you'd have maybe thought you'd landed in hell: the screams and calls of the exotic wildlife to your left, the clacking and groaning and cockney-accented French curses to your right.

At this time I was still in full-time employment, and only just beginning to think seriously about writing for money. One evening, I was the first to arrive at the piste, having come straight from work. As I tossed my cochonnet along the terrain, and causally practised my plomber and idly fingered my kiply, occasionally pausing to wipe my boules ferree on a beer towel, a young woman approached me and introduced herself. She was a freelance journalist, she said, doing an article for a leading women's magazine on unusual sports played by women.

There'd be some women along presently, I assured her. In the meantime, could I help? So, while she took photos of the empty pistes, and asked me the occasional unresearched question about boules ('Are your balls heavy? Do ladies prefer to play with lighter balls?'), I gradually edged the conversation round to her work.

It turned out that she was not much further forward in the writing game than I was. This sports feature of hers was, I realise in retrospect, a 'soft commission'; the editor hadn't said yes, she'd said 'Yeah, that could be worth doing. Depends on the pictures. Let me see it when you've finished, OK?'.

Shyly, I told her that I, too, 'did the odd bit of writing'.

She asked if I'd had any success. Proudly, I told her that I'd had several book reviews published in *Labour Weekly*. Humbly, I added that, of course, they didn't actually pay for reviews, but even so I –

'Ooh no you mustn't do that!' she interrupted, her cheeks flushed, her hair flapping, her breath coming in revolted gasps. 'Never work for free! They're just taking the mickey out of you – you'll never get anywhere if you work for free!' And she didn't talk to me again for the rest of the evening.

As it happened, the library where I then worked carried the magazine for which she was supposedly writing. I checked every issue for the next year: her piece on petanque never appeared; nor did anything else under her name.

But her terrible advice – never write for free – haunted me for years.

I have a friend who wrote a short story. It was a good story, by my reckoning, and I gave him the name and address of a respected magazine to which I suggested he submit it.

He did. The magazine accepted it. And when my friend found out that this magazine did not pay for stories, he withdrew it.

Nothing I could say to him – about the scarcity of paying markets, about the madness of turning down an opportunity to display your work in an influential setting – could dissuade him.

Why? He knew perfectly well that if he ever did find someone willing to pay for his story, the cheque would hardly cover his postage and photocopying costs. Even so, he would very happily have swapped unpaid publication in a prestigious place for meanly paid publication in a crappy mag. And we all know why: because getting paid proves that you're a *real* writer, instead of a *would-be* writer.

But look, I told him, *I'm* a real writer. I do it for a living. And I send stories out to non-paying markets and am delighted when they're accepted.

Exactly, he said. You do it for a living. You're got nothing to prove. But until I get paid for something, then I'm just another one of those millions of pathetic, self-deluding, mad scribblers that the world is so full of.

He was making a big mistake, and I tried to cure him of his error, but I couldn't blame him for it. It's a feeling we've all felt. As I said, the reaction of that stupid woman at the bouledrome troubled me for ages. Every time I wrote something for free, I'd feel a prickle of guilt, a horrible little tingle of shame.

I cured myself of this eventually – partly because I gradually realised that some of the best opportunities coming my way didn't involve direct payment. But I know that for many beginners in freelancing this is a huge mental obstacle.

If your local DIY superstore offered you a job as a Customer Care Assistant, but wasn't willing to pay you any wages, you should of course refuse. Refuse, and then set fire to the store. Working in a shop for nothing isn't work experience or career advancement, it's slavery. It is deregulation, competitiveness, global flexibility. It's bollocks.

But freelance writing is different, for all sorts of obvious and less obvious reasons. Not the least of which is that nobody has to be a writer, whereas if the dole office send you to Tools-U-Like, that's it – stack hacksaws or starve, boy.

Over the years, I've worked out some rules on working for free, and I've refined them and edited them and subbed them until I've got them down to just two simple laws.

1. Don't take a no-fee assignment if you suspect that by doing so you'd be doing someone else out of a fee. That's called scabbing, and it should carry the death penalty.

2. Always take a no-fee assignment if you believe that it gives you an opportunity to publish a worthwhile piece of work in a worthwhile outlet.

Remember that Freak Brothers motto? 'Dope will get you through times of no money better than money will get you through times of no dope.' For freelances, the rough equivalent is 'Work will get you through times of no money . . .'

Obviously if they can pay, they should pay, and so these rules only really apply to fanzines, the small press, small circulation journals and so on. And don't make the common mistake of supposing that getting work published without payment is necessarily easier than getting it published for money. (If you can't see why that should be, then give up now.)

Meanwhile, here's another list. I like lists, top tens, A to Zeds. They are easier to write, because you don't have to link everything together. And they take up more space, because of the layout. Lists are a sign of a lazy mind, and I know what that says about me, but I just can't be bothered to give a damn. This particular list concerns reviewing, and why it is worth doing even when you don't get paid for it. These items appear in no particular order, other than that which springs unconsciously from a twisted psyche.

1. The power of the plugger is something to be savoured. I once wrote a few paragraphs in a magazine column about an unusual one-man business. It helped me fill some space. Then I got a letter from the bloke who ran the business, saying that thanks to orders from my readers he wouldn't, after all, have to close down and go back on the dole. Of course, he may have been exaggerating – but if not, it means that I did more to bring down the unemployment figures in a few words than John Major managed in his entire career.

No matter how small the circulation of the paper you're writing for, if you match the story to the readers skilfully enough, you can have an astonishing effect . . . for good, or for (heh heh) *eee-villl* . . . One of the great pleasures of the freelance writer's life is being able to punish a company that's ripped you off by giving them some damaging free publicity.

2. Although many publications don't pay for book reviews, the reviewer usually gets to keep the books. I receive thousands of pounds worth of books every year. Traditionally, in broadcast and print journalism, staff hoard review copies and then finance their office Christmas party by selling them to book dealers. This is technically illegal (a phrase which means 'illegal'), and morally it's at least dubious – arguably, you are robbing authors of their royalties – and in any case, it's probably not worth risking on a small scale, though I must admit I've never heard of anybody being done for it.

On the other hand, if a book you were sent for free turns out five years later to be worth ten times what you didn't pay for it (like my copy of *Viz* No. 1, for instance), it's hard to imagine who you'd hurt by flogging it to a dealer.

Unfortunately, most review copies don't make it as collectibles, as they arrive by post and are therefore foxed to hell and back before you even open them.

Getting paid for book reviewing is just jam. The real wonder of it is that you can get almost any book you want simply by writing in to the publisher's press department and asking for it. And not just books; the other week I got a kit for making mini-cloches out of lemonade bottles. Free. Free!

3. Another one of my irritating little moral rules is that if you go to a pub or a club one night and there's a comedian on who you've never heard of, you should laugh as loud as you can and applaud solidly at the end, no matter how terrible he is, unless his job is one you think you could do better yourself, in which case I suppose you're entitled to your own opinion. As a reviewer, I like wherever possible to pick my own books, and to review, on the whole, books that I've enjoyed reading. If an editor selects your title for you, and sends you one that you loathe, then you must use your own judgement – ie have a look at the author's photo on the dust jacket, and if you don't like the look of him, give him a good kicking.

4. Occasionally, an editor will send you a book to review along with the significant message 'I thought you might have some fun with this one'. This is Latin for 'I wasn't at Oxford with this guy, so let's rip him to shreds', and must be considered a binding editorial instruction. I'm not keen on negative reviewing – it's fine for student paper poseurs, but in the grown-up world it seems to me an unproductive expenditure of time and effort. There again, these writer chappies always say they don't take any notice of reviews, don't they? And some of us have got bills to pay.

5. There's a story (*yes*, another one) about a bloke asked to review the latest paperback by a very fashionable writer; it had been universally praised in hardback. He read it and reviewed it honestly: it was OK, but nothing special, he couldn't really see what all the fuss was about. So he was a bit disturbed when his review appeared in print as a rave. He spoke to the books editor, who was unapologetic: 'Look, this chap is a genius, and that is official. When I received your review I assumed you'd made a mistake, and I corrected it'.

The chances of this story being true, I should say, are extremely low; the chances of it being 'true' on the other hand are extremely high. In its best version, it even has a punchline, where this review the reviewer never wrote is blurbed on the cover of the fashionable author's next outing – thus, when the fashionable author finally falls from favour, the reviewer is immortalised as the idiot who lionised an author who everyone now knows was rubbish.

6. Always do your own sending out of copies. Or, in English: suppose you've written a book review, which has been published in a newspaper. You want to make sure the publisher sees the review, so that they'll continue to send you free books. Don't assume either that the publisher will spot the review unprompted, or that the newspaper will remember to send the publisher a copy. Do it yourself. With almost every piece I have published, I check it for possible send-outs – is there someone, somewhere, who would benefit from seeing this article? Is there someone somewhere who it would be to my benefit to show this article to? (I said *English*, not grammarese.)

7. If you are sent a book to review and, having tried to read it you find that you have absolutely no idea what it's supposed to be about, what language it's written in, and how anyone could be excepted to review such a thing without at least six PhDs in subjects they didn't even do at your school, then you could always send it back with an apologetic note. On the other hand, if you're getting paid to review it, don't send it back; go down to the library, find some reviews of it in other papers, and crib those.

WASTING TIME: A BEGINNER'S GUIDE

Start off by writing fillers, the HowToWrites tell you. Gain in confidence, build a relationship with an editor, experience the early thrill of seeing your name in print. And, let's not forget, make £££s in your spare time.

Fillers can be useful, there's no denying that. Not so much as a step on a writing career ladder, but as a source of occasional bits of money for less effort than it takes to write a TV series. I've made money writing letters to the editor, and especially greetings card jokes – some companies pay well for the latter, and it's well worth your while finding out their requirements and rates.

But I refuse to believe that any freelance has ever gone from turning out 'Don't kids say the funniest things' for the kind of magazines you find in dentists' waiting rooms, to having a novel at number five in the paperback lists on both sides of the Atlantic simultaneously. (Having said that, some obvious break-in routes do work: many, if not most of those who make a good living out of TV and radio comedy shows did start by writing non-commissioned one-liners for *Weekending* and *The News Huddlines*.)

Still, unless you are amazingly lucky, there will never come a time in your writing life when you find yourself able with impunity to sneeze in the direction of a few quid. A few quid is always a thing worth having; believe me, as a freelance, the difference between earning five pounds and not earning five pounds on any given day is going to be a difference worth noting.

Like any market, you have to research it. If you're above such menial work, then (all together now) forget it. The readers' letters market has changed in the last few years. It's worth finding out also whether the paper pays by cheque or postal order; if the latter, you can write several letters a week under different names.

On the whole, though, originality is not necessary. There are several eternal favourites, letters which reappear in the letters columns all the time. 'Why don't delivery boys whistle any more' is rarely absent. The one about putting horse manure on rhubarb ('My grandson made us laugh when he said he preferred his with custard') is still going strong, as is 'Why is it that as soon as the dentist has got your mouth full of equipment he asks where you're going for your holidays?'. A popular item in recent years has been the one about all the characters in TV serials who are referred to but never seen on screen, and how this is 'clearly a case for Mulder and Scully off of TV's *The X-Files*'.

But of course the unwhistling delivery boy might itself be a bit of fun, inserted by the young journalists who run such columns, and who are either seeking a bit of light relief, or else are trying to distance themselves from what they perceive as proletarian banality, so that they can tell their friends 'Yes, I do run a tabloid letters page, but it's like dead ironic, y'know?'.

HOW TO TAKE UMBRAGE

One of my favourite HowToWrite perennials is 'Rejections, And What We Can Learn From Them'. Oh, *yeah*!

The only thing you can learn from a rejection is this: they don't want you. And why should they? This is a buyer's market, remember.

If there *is* anything you learn from rejections, then you're in trouble. If you need to learn not to send poems to a magazine that never uses poems, or not to send 10,000 word essays to magazines that specialise exclusively in haiku, then *give up now*!

Other than that what can rejection teach you? What hidden meaning can you tease out of it? None at all. It means exactly what it says on the rejection slip: 'This doesn't suit our needs at the moment'. It means that there is no reason for them to accept your stuff unless they happen to want it at that particular moment. They don't need reasons for rejecting anything, beyond the obvious one that the ratio of Stuff to Space (let alone the Stuff to Dosh ratio) is not in your favour.

This can be scientifically expressed as follows:

X = (Y divided by 1,000,000,000,000,000,000,000) where X = the space available for Stuff, and Y = the amount of Stuff in circulation at any given moment.

Don't waste your eyesight trying to read the entrails of a rejection. Honestly, you'd be better off having your palm read. A rejection means 'No', and that's all it means. The only thing we can learn from it is that we'd better get down the post office before it closes because we've run out of stamps yet again.

(Bet there's a monster queue at the stamp counter. Bet you anything you like it's pension day.)

I STOLE THIS BIT FROM THE COMPLETE GUIDE TO SUCCESSFUL WRITING BY IVAN OVERDRAFT

One of the commonest questions put to the ex-spurts in their ex-spurt advice columns in the HowToWrite mags is 'How can I establish copyright on my articles, stories, poems, jokes and life story?' to which the ex-spurt always replies that, in point of actual fact, copyright is automatically established on all creative work at the moment of creation, but that to establish *proof* of copyright you should post a copy to yourself in a sealed envelope and don't open it until Perry Mason gives you the signal.

Which is all true. And which is all balls.

Do these people honestly believe that their deranged scribblings are in danger of being heisted by – well, by who? Editors, subs, other writers, printers? Beelzebub and all his legions?

Yes, they do honestly believe that. Because, you see, they are mad. Mad and egomaniacal. That's why, every time they write a poem about a cat, or every time they come up with a sure-fire winner of a TV hit format ('Dear Sir, I hereby submit my latest idea for a new panel game. It would involve a number of witty celebrities being spontaneously amusing about a particular subject. I shall leave you to work out the lesser details yourself. Please make cheques payable to Hugh Jidiot, my pen name'), they always post themselves a carbon in a heavy duty envelope and, upon its receipt (I'd like you to witness this, Mr Postie), they solemnly, ceremoniously install it, its majestic seal ostentatiously unbroken, into the sacred Cupboard Of Copyright in the fabled Spare Bedroom Of Genius.

Where it sits with all the others forever, their seals eternally intact, because nobody, if we all live to be a thousand and one, is ever going to try and pinch any poor bastard's poem about cats.

The only seals that ever do get penetrated, as it happens, are the ones concerning panel games. TV and radio companies spend a fair bit of their time replying to mad letters, sent by registered post and lumpy with sealing wax, in which Hugh Jidiot attempts to recoup his stolen royalties, and which usually end: 'PS: Why did you change the setting of the quiz? I specified "on Concorde", not "in a grotty studio". PPS: And couldn't you get a decently-spoken announcer, instead of that dreadful woman with her garbled vowel sounds? And will someone Please tell the so-called Chairman that there was a time when so-called Comedians didn't need to resort to sex, violence, filth, disrespectfulness and Language in order to get Cheap Laughs'.

Unsuccessful writers are always paranoid about plagiarism. Look: nobody's going to steal your stuff, all right? Because first of all your stuff is *shit* and they are far more likely to steal your orange-and-banana pattern *curtains*, and secondly that just isn't how it works. People in the scribblebiz don't want your stuff. They've got their own stuff. They've got more stuff piled up than they can ever hope to know what to do with. It isn't stuff that's in short supply, as we've already established, it's slots and dosh.

OK, it does happen. There was a case in the papers not long ago about a bestselling romance novelist who turned out to have lifted great long chunks of lovey-stuff from the bestselling romance novels of one of her chief rivals. (I think her name was Miss Subtlecow, or something.) Anyway, it turned out that the reason she'd done this wasn't that she was a plagiarist but that (according to the newspaper reports at least) she was ill. It was one of those cry-for-help thangs, y'know? (That would have been Hitler's excuse if they'd ever caught him. 'I voz short und titchy! I needed to attract people's attention!')

Being rich, female and American she's almost certainly in therapy right now, going to a self-help group called Copiers Anonymous LA, which is probably being sued by a group in Chicago which claims to have thought of the name first, just as I am now being sued by seventy-three newspaper humorists who say they thought of that joke first.

My defence will be the traditional defence of the comedy writer throughout history: all jokes are old. If they smell a bit, the thing to do is to take them one stage further, and then another, until you can feel them starting to freshen up again.

Plagiarism? Plagiarism! You should be so lucky! Believe me, getting your stuff copied is the very last thing you should be worrying about. Getting it *published*, so that people have an opportunity to plagiarise it – now, that's worth worrying about.

Relax, because this works both ways. Well, how do you imagine anything ever gets to be written? Shakespeare didn't invent any of his stories, nor did Chaucer, nor did the various and divers authors of the Bible, nor, in a sense, did Stan Lee. Nothing is original, so if you see something you fancy – a character, a gag, a plot device, a location – take it. Take it, go on, take it. Rework it, mess it around, give it a quick respray, change the plates, scratch out the serial number, mix and match it. It's like shoplifting; they can only do you for it if they've got you on the security video, or if they catch you on the pavement with the goods in your pocket.

You are never going to write anything original. You are never going to create anything wholly new. If you did, you would be in direct contravention of Newtonian laws of matter, which would cause infinite quantities of quantum miniverses to spring into being around the nib of your mouse. And c'mon honey, you *know* that's not what you want.

LEARNING TO SUBMIT

Presentation is one of those filler subjects that the writers' mags are always full of. When they can't find anything to write about, or anyone to write about it, they drag out the old presentation number, touch it up a bit (ie make sure it doesn't contain too many references to pre-decimal currency) and there you are: a page filled.

If you were the sort of person who believed what you read in the HowToWrites, you might well grow up with a crippling complex, unable to insert a margin or staple a corner or double-space a para, even in the loving sanctity of the marital bed, for fear of getting it wrong and thus inviting the scorn and contempt of properly turned-out writers the world over.

If presentation is something you find yourself worrying about, then you're fairly bloody clearly in the wrong job, aren't you? I mean, really: if you're incapable of finding out or even figuring out the standard, mostly common-sense ways in which manuscripts are presented, and allying them with a few very basic rules about spelling and punctuation, then forget it!

Obviously, if you're used to writing magazine articles and you then switch to TV scripts you're going to want to make sure you know what the differences are in layout, but other than that . . . listen, 'presentation' is something the HowTos go on and on about *because* it's a nothing subject, so they don't need to know anything about writing in order to know enough to write their thirty-seventh 'Correct Presentation: Half the Battle!' article.

The only place you'll find editors and publishers who are as obsessed with presentation as are the HowTos is among certain sections of the small press in the USA. I've often sent off for writers' guidelines from small American mags, and received back what reads more like the *New York Times* journal of house style: insanely detailed, minutely precise instructions on the use of commas, paper clips and permissible paper GSM bands.

Word to the wise: never waste time submitting to or subscribing to a magazine which offers more than a quarter page of presentation instructions: from long experience I can guarantee that no such magazine has ever made it to a third issue, or to a circulation greater than forty-two, or to a page count higher than twenty.

Well, hell, that's Americans for you. That's small press egos for you. But real-life publishers don't seem to give a monkey's. As a book reviewer, I am sometimes sent a photocopy of the author's original MS, if the publisher is so excited about a particular property that she wants to get the hype rolling soonest, baby, and she can't wait for the page proofs. And I'll tell you something: those MSS are invariably incorrectly margined, wrongly indented, criminally spelt, eccentrically punctuated, on unorthodox-sized sheets of dissidently-weighted paper with frankly effete line spacing.

Ah-ha, but the twist (we do *love* a twist, us, don't we?) is that this lack of presentational care irritates me, and, though I try not to let it, can't help but have a subconsciously negative effect on my reading and reviewing of the book.

Therefore, let us not sneer at presentation; let us, instead, provide a few basic presentation rules, to satisfy the people who bought this book thinking it was a HowToWrite and are feeling ripped off by now.

1. Write on one side of the paper only, rather than between the leaves of a fir cone.

2. Do not use crayon.

3. Do not paint 'pig's bum' over your MS in creosote in such a way as to obscure the text.

4. Do not burn your MS and then send the ashes to the editor in an urn. It is far better instead to send a clean copy of your article or story.

5. Most major publishing houses will not consider MSS written in a secret code known only to you and your cousin. Unfair, maybe, but there it is.

6. Etc.

7. Always leave generous margins, otherwise you will never enjoy a satisfying marital relationship in the physical department.

5: 22 things you already know

MORE BLOODY LISTS At school when you were taught to swim did you ever have a PE teacher who on your first pool visit gathered the class round and said things like 'Now then, a few basic rules before we start. Number One, do not kneel on the bottom of the swimming pool with your mouth open breathing for several minutes at a time. Number Two, do not – *Jenkins, are you listening? This might be important, boy, that might even be why I'm saying it, you ever thought of that?* – do not jump into the deep end with a large piece of concrete sellotaped to your head. Number Three, standing on people in the pool while they emit slowly diminishing air bubbles is strictly forbidden. Number Twenty-Seven . . .'

The next few pages are a bit like that PE teacher. The reason he told you those insultingly obvious things was, hard as this is to believe, that at some time in his career, or in his mentor's career, someone *had* actually stood on a classmate's head in a municipal baths and drowned him purely because he had never been told not to.

(That isn't true of course. The real reason the PE teacher said those things was because he was a PE teacher, he couldn't help himself.)

Try not to be insulted by these pages. But do try to let them sink into your subconscious. In fact, stand on their heads until they have sunk good and deep. Because here they come – the official rules for writers to live by . . .

1. Never send your only copy of a piece of work through the post. Not even by registered post or security van. Never. And, yes, I realise that no intelligent person would ever do such a thing. I did it myself once, and when my then writing partner found out he had to be physically pulled off my throat by four policemen, a fireman, and an Albanian Buddhist wearing a bright orange kangaroo costume. (The Albanian Buddhist wasn't actually with the emergency services, he just happened to be passing and held a strong personal aversion to violence. I am grateful to him to this day.)

2. Do not keep only floppy disc copies or only hard disc copies or only paper copies. Keep hard, floppy and paper copies of everything. And keep them in separate places.

3. Just to make sure I am labouring this point in sufficiently condescending detail, when I say 'don't keep them in the same place', I mean keep them in different places. Separately. Yah?

4. Make disc copies of everything, regularly update them, and give them to a friend for safekeeping (you're going to hate me for this, but NB: a friend who does not live in the same house as you do). The number of people who have lost their files to fires, floods or burglaries, and have been driven to madness not by the loss itself but by the friends who say 'But surely you kept backups?'. . . well, it don't hardly bear thinkin' about. Because the only honest reply to that question is 'Yes, yes, of course I kept backups, they were three feet away from the originals'.

You may not believe people can be that stupid. You certainly don't believe you can be that stupid. Until it happens to you. If we're going to be completely honest here, it ought to be said that never mind ignoring good advice – even after writing this chapter, even after it's been published, the likelihood of some of these disasters befalling me, through my own negligence, will not yet have reached zero.

See, that's how stupid and complacent we all are at times. The times in question being, roughly, the times between birth and death.

5. Always wear a belt, no matter how tight your trousers are, because if you trip during a hike and gash your leg, you can use the belt as a makeshift tourniquet until qualified medical help arrives.

6. Sign up with an accountant as soon as you start earning a second income (or, if you're unemployed, a first income) from writing. A lot of writers don't bother, and it's true that many writing books include chapters on how to manage your income tax, and it's true that you probably could do a lot of it yourself. It's also true that accountants cost money (although their fees are themselves tax deductible). But tax is a dangerous area, and it is definitely best to be in professional hands right from the start – there is simply so much that the accountant knows that you don't even know you don't know; stuff you've never dreamed of. It's said that in music hall days, comedians were able to claim their cigarettes against tax, because they used them to time their acts. I've no idea whether that's true, or quite why I've mentioned it here except that it's a little piece of trivia I've always wanted to use somewhere – but whatever you do, get an accountant as soon as you can. And make sure you get one who knows something about freelancing; ask other writers for recommendations.

7. Pin a rota to your wall to make sure you change your trousers regularly. If you're forgetting to change your vest and pants then you're ill and should see your GP, but trousers are so easy to forget, it's easy to wear them for three or four months without a break, because, being a writer, you never go anywhere or see any one.

8. If possible have your writing desk by a window and outside the window have a bird table or hanging bag of peanuts. Bird-watching will force you to look away from your computer screen frequently, thus saving your eyesight and preventing having your brain burnt out by the radiation. Or at least, postponing it until you've finished your book.

9. One of the most important pieces of advice I could ever possibly give you is coming up right now. It's not an easy rule to live by, and I can't pretend that I have managed to live by it myself, or even got anywhere near it, but if you do listen to this and if you do adopt it then I know that you will be grateful to me for the rest of your life. It is simply this: have something in your life that you don't write about. Something that's real, that's for you, not just for material.

A few years ago, I got quite loopy about quiz machines. It got so that I couldn't pass a pub at any time of day without going in to check what sort of quizzer it offered. Financially, this wasn't a problem, since my friends and I soon discovered that, if we adopted a disciplined approach to which machines we played and how and when, we were usually able to pay for a modest night out (beer, curry and quiz machine stake) with our winnings.

The problem only came when it occurred to me that I was spending nearly all my time quiz-machining instead of writing. And furthermore, that if I could find some way to earn from quiz-machining, then I'd be able to call my playing 'research' and would thus be justified in spending all, instead of nearly all, my time on the flashing buttons.

I wrote three-quarters of a bad radio play, in which quiz machining was a metaphor for . . . something, I can't remember what. The play was called *B! B! Damn It The Answer Is B! See? Eh? You Idiot! I TOLD YOU To Press B!*.

I worked up two-thirds of a radio panel game format. I spent weeks researching, and even starting to write, a consumer's guide to quiz machining. That could actually have been a very valuable piece of work, if it wasn't that long before I could finish it the gaming machine industry suddenly realised that people were regularly winning more than they lost on quiz machines, and responded to this outrage by replacing the machines with a new generation of games which only paid out when there was a Z in the month.

Quiz machines were no fun any more, the spell was broken, my fever receded, and I went back to work. And the only money I ever made out of quiz machines were the coins that came a-klunkin' out of the belly of the beast itself.

I can't have a hobby, an interest, a passion, a solace, without writing about it or trying to write about it. Thus, I'm never fully off duty. If you're wise (which I doubt) you'll aim to develop better hobby habits.

10. Remember that long words can be shorter than short words. One precisely employed albeit unfamiliar term can take the place of a couple of lines of every-day waffle. When you're editing down a 2,000 word draft to an 800 word piece, this can be important. Remember also that this is the only legitimate reason for using unfamiliar synonyms.

11. Keep a copy of – *yes*, we're back on keeping copies – keep a copy, I say, of everything you ever write, not just the stuff you write for publication. Putting this book together I have gone back through my immaculate filing system to cannibalise, for instance, letters I wrote to friends five years ago. Be a bureaucrat, not an artist; opponents of list-making may appear fashionable and middle-class, but they are also people of low self-confidence, sheeplike intellect, and invariably suffer from an incurable inability to create.

12. If you can't get your book published, then pay someone to publish it for you. Well, why not? Why the hell not? A lot of the prejudice against so-called vanity presses (as if vanity were not an integral part of any publishing process) comes from the writers' advice industry trying to make itself sound big and tough and grown-up and serious and respectable; trying to sound as if the people who write for writers' mags are writers, rather than pathetic tossers.

What those magazines should be doing is providing consumer reports on individual vanity presses. It's perfectly true that you are likely to be ripped off by author-pays outfits, but only because nobody regulates the bastards.

There is no legitimate reason why you shouldn't pay for it, if you're not getting any in the usual way. I myself have a couple of slim volumes which I know will never be bought by any proper publisher, but which I also know I could sell two or three hundred copies of given a chance; more importantly, books which I would love to see in print because they mean something to me. I've never had the money to do anything about it, but if I ever have I will. Like I said, why the hell not?

Vanity publishing is only a few steps removed from full self-publishing – a process open only to those who know what they're doing, and which is not at all looked down upon these days.

If you do get conned by a vanity press, then frankly you are almost certainly an idiot with no one to blame but yourself, since your distress can only mean that you failed to demand and follow up on references, you failed to shop around, you failed to read the contract, you failed to think before buying an expensive product. Which, if you remember, is how you ended up with that pink jacket, not to mention the souvenir Complete Tolkein boxed set bound in puppy leather.

13. Never make the mistake of believing a magazine's own image of itself. Religious papers are usually staffed by atheists and homosexuals, men's porno titles are edited by heterosexual women, and overworked subs cram their mouths with tuna sandwiches as they edit the copy on vegetarian magazines. Now I come to think of it, I'm not entirely sure what value this knowledge is likely to be – to you or to me. But knowledge is always useful, so keep it in mind, eh?

14. When you're working on a collaboration with a friend, or potential friend, always make the money deal 50/50, no matter who's done what in the way of work, because otherwise there will surely be a falling out, even if it's an unspoken one, and it just isn't worth it for a few quid.

15. Always remember you're trying to impress an editor, not a reader. I once wrote a big piece for a big paper and the chap who'd commissioned it was generous in his praise of its subtle structure, its intellectual depth and its bold ideas. So when I saw it in print, I was initially horrified to discover that he'd cut out all the stuff he'd been most enthusiastic about. Gradually it occurred to me that really, it didn't matter. The editor had cut the piece for reasons of his own – to save space, to please his boss, to fit in with his paper's political stance or advertising profile – but never mind. He'd read it, he'd liked it, and that meant that he'd use me again. The fact that his readers never got to experience the full wonder of my brilliance was irrelevant, because they weren't the ones who decided whether or not to buy my stuff.

16. Join the public library; obvious even by the standards of this chapter, I know, but it can't be said too often.

17. Keep a diary. Of all the things I wish I'd done, keeping a diary is near the top of the list. I wish that when I first thought 'I wish I'd kept a diary' I'd started keeping a diary then. I wish that having written the last two lines, I'd start keeping a diary now.

18. Note that the first duty of the revolutionary writer is to provide readers with the means of imaginative escape from the awfulness of everyday life and the exhaustions of the class struggle. Forget the clever stuff: nothing so refreshes a cadre ready for the battles of tomorrow than a good, thick, enveloping dollop of spirit-enhancing fantasy.

19. Cultivate your prejudices, because you'll find enormous amounts of material there.

20. All my early, pre-professional writing was done on bright green paper, because a friend's brother-in-law at the pub nicked it for me from work. He hardly knew me; he just wanted to do a young fellow a favour. This *isn't* something you already know, obviously (or, presumably), but I wanted to mention it because it just makes me happy whenever I remember it.

21. If a magazine (TV company, whatever) asks you to lend it a prop, don't do it. For instance, you've written a feature on fortune telling scams and the picture editor rings up to ask if he can borrow your crystal ball for the photos, to save him having to go out and buy one. Don't do it. Make an excuse. 'Sorry, but disfortunately my crystal ball got broked this morning when a piece of Korean spy satellite fell upon it.' If you lend them your crystal ball, you will never get it back – there is a Law of Offices which makes it physically impossible for this to happen – and what's worse, if you keep asking for it back you will drive them all mad and they will come to hate you and think you are a pathetic nutter, obsessed with getting his crystal ball back that nobody can remember seeing in the first place and which in any case they never did use as a photo prop due to they cut your piece to make way for a chatline ad.

22. Try not to be hip, try not to be cool, try not to be fashionable or trendy or in the swim or up to the minute. Try to write as if, you know, you actually gave a damn. Once a month make a list of the ten most modish words and phrases current in the media, so that you can be sure you don't use any of them by accident.

So, there you are. I hope you haven't learned something useful from the above, because it's all stuff you should have known long ago.

Before we leave this sector, I should like to point out that there are two significant differences between me and the PE teacher. One, I don't have a Gym-and-Geog Stiffcate. And two, doctors did not consider removal of the brain and its replacement with a tin of ravioli to be a viable treatment option in my case.

I received a personalised form letter from the local Tory candidate during the last general election, the first sentence of which was 'I am writing to you at this stage of my Campaign'. Full stop.

HOW TO BE SEMI-LITERATE

So much for the party of traditional educational values: here we have a redundant Capital Initial, and a mind-blowing statement of the obvious.

Semi-literacy has become our culture's lingua franca. Officialdom, commerce, royalty, every institution in the Western world speaks and writes with a level of precision and clarity which, on a civilised planet, would scarcely be acceptable from a chimpanzee.

Or anyway, that's my excuse.

Meanwhile, here are just a very few of the *clichés you should die rather than use*:

1. 'To die for' (meaning quite nice).

2. 'Just when you thought it was safe to . . .' I bet that was one was quite amusing during the first six years after the shark film's release.

3. This opening paragraph, from a feature piece in a national newspaper, reads like the UK entry to the Cliché Olympics: 'Love it or loathe it, there's no avoiding it. *This Life*, BBC2's sophisticated soap about a bunch of twenty-something lawyers, is *the* must-see show for the *Friends* generation'. Well, kids – how many clichés did you spot?

4. 'a la' meaning in the manner of.

5. As well as modish clichés, there are those that remain popular for generations; for instance describing someone who is surprised by something as looking 'like a startled rabbit'. How many people, I wonder, have actually seen a startled rabbit? You wouldn't have long to look at it, would you? If it was startled, I mean, it wouldn't just stand there, looking startled, while you sketched it. I suppose you could undertake some private research; buy yourself a rabbit, keep it in a hutch, and then just as it was beginning to get used to the quiet life, you could go up to it and say 'Guess what? Tony Blair's been voted the world's sexiest human being' and swiftly take a sneaky Polaroid of its facial expression, for future reference. But it might be easier – I say *might be easier* – just to think up a new form of words.

6. 'Like a [something] on speed [or acid, or E, or whatever].' Another cliché which was probably pretty cool about forty years ago.

7. Opening an article with 'SEX! There that got your attention, didn't it!' or 'So your esteemed editor asked yours truly to come up with 500 witty words on sausages. Well, never one to duck a challenge I said OK, so here goes. Sausages have been known to mankind since at least the time of the Ancient Babylonians . . .'

8. 'I hear you cry.' This one really does deserve the death penalty. 'Sausages in Ancient Babylon – but what has this got to do with me, I hear you cry. Well! Quite a lot, as it turns out!'

9. At all costs avoid opening humorous pieces with 'It can happen anywhere' as in 'It can happen anywhere. One minute you're sitting at your favourite Babylonian restaurant enjoying some ancient sausages, when suddenly – Mr Flash Git at the next table whips out his mobile phone and starts chattering away. We've all been there. Irritating isn't it? But what can I do about it, I hear you cry . . .'

10. Don't use words like 'git', 'shag', 'bonk'. There is perhaps nothing in the world less cool than using terms which were until recently taboo but which are now, as a result of TV exposure, trendily acceptable.

11. I accept that all this is to a large extent a matter of taste, but I hope we're all agreed that the word 'lady' should be banned by an act of parliament. During the last general election, a woman in Exeter told a newspaper reporter that she would not be voting Labour because 'the Labour man is gay. I'm a family lady and I think there's too much of that sort of thing going on'.

12. Never use any phrase, word, or even vowel sound that you have heard used on a radio or television consumer programme.

While we're at it, here are some ideas that aren't worth having, some articles that aren't worth writing and some jokes that aren't worth cracking:

1. 'Not long ago, admitting to a liking for sci-fi was akin to [blah blah, cliché cliché, nerd, anorak, blah]. But now today however all that has changed. Yes! Holy spaceships! It's true! Sci-fi is now cool!'

2. 'Since the black box always survives crashes, why not make the whole aeroplane out of the same material?'

3. 'How come people who claim to have been reincarnated were always King Arthur or Cleopatra in their previous life? How come nobody was ever a humble spear-carrier?'

4. SF stories in which only two people are left alive after a nuclear holocaust and in the last line of the story we discover that their names are . . . Adam and Eve.

5. 'I moved from London to the country in search of rural peace and quiet, but now I'm coming back to the city – fleeing from small town small mindedness, cultural deprivation, blah blah.' I've seen this article about seventy times in the last five years.

Why *not* write clichéd articles if they continue to sell? Good question, and one that I can't answer for you, I'm afraid, you'll have to figure that one out for yourself. One tip I will pass on, though, is that you can often make a few quid writing articles about how clichéd the clichéd articles are. At least, you can until those articles themselves become clichéd.

And here's the simple guide to avoiding clichés: when you're writing a sentence and you hear a cliché approaching, blast it with the old reverser ray. The reason clichés are inefficient writing, as well as merely irritating, is that readers don't read them, don't register them; they skim them. All you've got to do, to render your flattened sentences tactual again, is change one word, or reverse one phrase. I kid you not, it's as easy as falling off a dog.

HOW TO NURTURE YOUR IGNORANCE

Just before I gave up dayjobbing for the freelance demi-life, I had a job which partly involved reading periodicals and cutting things out of them. I won't go into more detail than that, because the pictures in your head are sure to be better than the truth.

This activity was called scanning, and it became the basis of a habit which has proved invaluable ever since. For all kinds of writing, but perhaps for imaginative even more than factual writing, it is necessary for the writer to receive as varied a range of influences and input as possible. You can't possibly write decent SF if all you ever read is the *Guardian*. Unfortunately, plenty of people *do* write crime fiction although all they ever read is the *Telegraph*.

The real meat in life is hidden in nooks and crannies, that's why you have to read like an archaeologist, not like a newsreader. Babies swallow whatever puréed veg they're fed by various adults, and that's fine for babies. But us grown-ups, we prefer corn on the cob, which involves getting your busy, active, seeking teeth *right in there*, into all those little tasty crevices, and then using your tongue to flick out the bits from between your gums. Grown-ups don't swallow things whole, we need to chew them a bit first.

Part of the answer to 'where do ideas come from' is the truism that they come from looking at everyday objects from an unfamiliar angle – and while mind-altering drugs are probably better for you than newspapers, they are also much more expensive, so after you've changed your regular pub, your route to work and your luncheon arrangements, change your reading habits, too.

The rapidly and radically narrowing range of expressible opinions and tellable truths in contemporary Britain is creating a press consensus more rigidly defined and vigorously enforced than any seen in this part of the world for several generations. This means we have to seek further afield for our chewy bits. Subscribe to as many obscure journals as possible, especially those on subjects you're not interested in. If you're an arts fan, read the city pages instead. As for which mainstream papers you read, it doesn't really matter, since they are all much of a muchness, provided only that it isn't the paper you grew up reading. *How* you read is more important.

Scanning isn't exactly reading, and it isn't exactly skimming. You'll have to devise your own technique, and the only clue I can give you is that when it's done properly, scanning is a kind of methodical serendipity. When you're scanning, you know what you're looking for, but you won't know it when you see it. And – well, and other clever-sounding paradoxes. (Flicking through a periodical which you usually read anyway doesn't count as scanning, nor does market research, when you buy a title to study it for possible sales.)

Every magazine and paper that comes your way, including stained ones found in railway carriages, and freebies left dangling out of your letter box in the rain while you're away for three weeks, must be scanned. If you're doing it properly it'll take maybe an hour out of a full-time writer's day, every day (if you've still got a day job, lock yourself in the bog and do it there), and it will quickly become very boring and will mostly seem like a terrible waste of time. But I swear to you, I've made £££s directly and indirectly from bits of work generated directly or indirectly by scanning. It really is where I get my ideas from, madam, and no, that's not why they're such bad ones.

Eclecticism is the key; all the mainstream papers are the same.

You might sometimes wonder, for instance, why all those newspapers which have books pages review exactly the same books in the same week. Wouldn't you think, in a competitive market, it would be in their interests to attract readers by offering something different?

One answer I think is that broadsheet readers do not tend to be people of an independent set of mind. They are the type who believe that there is in life a kind of national curriculum for adults, a set of things – 'issues', as they tend to call them – which they need to know about, in art, politics, books, cinema, ideas, food, fashions. One paper may suit them better than another, but this is just a minor matter of flavouring, or more likely of habit. The *Telegraph* reader wants, or thinks he needs, to be superficially aware of precisely the same set of 'issues' as does the *Guardian* or *Independent* reader.

There is nowadays no significant difference between the broadsheets and the tabloids – the tablecloths and the chip wrappers – other than that chip wrappers tend to be staffed by professional journalists, while the tablecloths are staffed by people who were at boarding school with the editor's sister. For a couple of years, I took the *Mirror* and the *Telegraph*; the *Mirror* for a quick digest of the news, and the *Telegraph* for the fact that under a special offer designed to make its circulation look unnaturally rosy it was available at just one pound a week for seven day's papers.

These two papers are to all intents and purposes identical (right down to the half-naked women, which the *Telegraph* carries daily on page two and which it calls 'fashion news') . If you don't believe me, do a couple of experiments (but remember to ask Mummy or Daddy before trying anything which involves sharp scissors, glue or semi-automatic firearms). Try reading a few headlines or teasers from these two papers, or any others, and invite your jolly party guests to guess which paper you're reading from.

Better still (though less jolly as a party game, perhaps), measure and compare (as a proportion of total paperage) the space given in the *Mail* and the *Independent* to any story or subject you choose.

Or alternatively, you could just *take my bleeding word for it, you bastard!* What do you think I'm gonna do, lie to you?

The broadsheets no longer exist; they've become broadloids. Of course there are still differences of tone. In what looked alarmingly like self-parody the *Telegraph,* a couple of years ago, devoted the bulk of its front page to an opinion poll which claimed to show that most people knew nothing about the British Empire, while half of page three was taken by the revelation that a former *Mastermind* semi-finalist had once had anorexia. Yes, the

Telegraph is a tabloid in all but size, and pretensions. It's a tabloid for snobs, obviously, and for people who lack the intellectual equipment to decode the *Sun*. A typical *Telegraph* headline: 'I Was Eaten By A Hyena'.

It used to be an important paper for writers to scan, as what little news it did cover was mostly made up of just the sort of nonsense we yearn for: daft boffins, incompetent crooks, Home Counties forteanism. But today, for commercial reasons largely, it has abandoned its old eccentricity and is no longer snobby and weird. Now it's just snobby. Every couple of weeks it does a 'news story' about a public schoolboy running away from school, and turning up in Florida or Barbados. This will occupy the front page and two or three pages inside. The rest of the 'news' concerns fox-hunting, and how much the foxes enjoy it, and a bit about property prices in Provence.

You think I'm making this up, don't you? I'm not, I'm just reminding you that to become and remain a successful scanner, you must keep your eyes open and your feet moving. Dance like a butterfly, read like a bee.

The tablecloths use the chip wrappers to break stories which would upset their insider relationships if *they* broke them; then the poshies can cover exactly the same story in twice as much disgusting detail, under the rubric of 'Shame Of The Evil Tabloids – full details page 2, 3, 4, 5, 6, 7, 8, 9 and centre spread'.

The *Morning Star* is, I would suggest, an indispensable part of the freelance's regular reading. The *Star* (then called the *Daily Worker*) was founded by the Communist Party of Great Britain in 1930, but ownership was transferred after World War Two to a co-op, the People's Press Printing Society, thus creating the first national daily owned by its readers. Today, the *Star* is the world's only avowedly socialist daily paper published in the English language. Membership of the co-op which owns and runs the paper is open to all its readers. Its survival through decades of advertising boycotts, government suppression, and political unfashionability sometimes seems like a miracle, but is in fact largely due to the die-hard determination of its readers and their fund-raising committees.

Its politics are far broader today than in the days of the Soviet Union, but irrespective of your own politics, it is the *Star*'s independence (exclusion, even) from the transnational consensus that makes it as useful to writers as it is to trades union activists.

It is in its foreign coverage that the difference is most dramatic. The consensus press only covers New York, Berlin, Brussels and Washington. Anywhere else is exotic, third world, covered only by jokey, 'fancy that' paragraphs from the news agencies: funny little oriental men doing funny little oriental things involving alcohol and red hot pokers; funny little brown chaps starving; hairy little black chaps killing each other. If you want to know what's happening in the world (and you do), not just in Cuba, Brazil, Vietnam, but in rural USA, eastern Germany or suburban Canada – anywhere outside the AmEx pool of light in which the mainstream papers' correspondents dwell, and remembering that for most of us today our own country is a foreign land, too – you have to read the *Morning Star*.

There are many other reasons for reading the *Star* (its Monday books page is widely held to be one of the best in Britain), but I don't want you to think I'm trying to sell you something here, so I'll content myself with reiterating the main one: that the *Morning Star* isn't the other papers. The *Star* is available on order from all newsagents, or by postal subscription from the paper's London headquarters. It's now available online at www. morningstaronline.co.uk.

The number of titles (not only overtly political titles, either) which are no longer stocked by the tiny handful of news trade distributors who now have total control over what you are and are not allowed to read in the UK is alarming. Monopoly owners and monopoly distributors between them are steadily eroding any pretence at press freedom.

The news media doesn't exist to report news – perhaps it never did. It's no coincidence that the media's favourite subject is the media. Get your stopwatch out, and you may be amazed at what proportion of a day's TV and radio news is news coverage of news coverage.

Have you noticed how the prize crossword in Saturday's paper is always easier than the non-prize crosswords during the week? No, neither have I particularly, but I'll bet it's true, because the papers want as many people as possible to enter their competitions, thus allowing them to build up a commercially valuable database of names and addresses. Newspapers today aren't really in the news business; they are just marketing tools.

If you ever get the opportunity to read a newspaper account of a subject about which you know something, it can be an interesting exercise. You will discover that every verifiable fact in the article is wrong. I know that sounds like an exaggeration, but all I can say is – try it. A supposedly upmarket colour supp recently ran a feature about my home town. I stopped reading after the first sentence, when I saw that they'd managed to place the town in the wrong county. They got the region more or less right, though, which is actually pretty good going by journalistic standards.

The mass media lie or get it wrong or both on every possible occasion. On the morning of Princess Di's death, BBC Radio 4 reported that the streets of London were thronged with stunned people, many of them weeping openly. It looked as if a bomb had dropped, one reporter claimed. Every business was closed, traffic was at a standstill. This was pure invention – this was the consensus media attempting (not entirely successfully as it turned out) to create events, rather than to report them; but that's undoubtedly how that day will be written up in the history books.

But we (all right then, *I*) must be wary of attributing too much solidarity and conspiratorial invincibility to the news consensus. Its servants slip up with delightful frequency. For instance, when the Scottish electorate voted in a referendum in favour of devolution, the *Telegraph* (which was anti-devolution) reported 'There were no street parties, no impromptu celebrations . . .' while the TV news (which was pro-devolution) showed film of street parties, impromptu celebrations and general *al fresco* champagne-swigging.

Remember there are never any circumstances whatsoever under which any mainstream newspaper tells the truth.

Therefore, when you write for newspapers, make it up. Lie, lie, lie. It's easier, it's better, it's more ethical. And it means you can stay in bed all day.

If it's good enough for them, it's good enough for you. Have you ever tried phoning someone who works on a national daily? They are never in the office. And why? Because they are at home in bed, making it all up and then emailing it through. There isn't a single reporter in this country who has ever actually interviewed anyone, let alone attended a third division football match in person.

Well, would you?

It is a well-known fact that the most complete waste of time which a freelance can engage in is sending unsolicited manuscripts to national newspapers. National newspapers do not use unsolicited contributions. They don't. However, and just to underline the theme of total confusion which runs through this book like a corkscrewed spine, I have sold several pieces to the nationals in exactly this manner.

For instance, I wrote a piece about how to grow garlic, and sent it in to the *Independent*'s gardening editor. It was used almost immediately. I didn't know, but as it turned out the paper's regular gardening correspondent was on holiday. I have never since sold another piece on gardening to that paper. Perhaps its gardening correspondent has never had another holiday? In any case, rules are not made to be broken (obviously; why would anybody make a rule in order for it to be broken? Doesn't make sense), and the rule is: do not waste your time sending unsolicited stuff to newspapers. One gardening piece (and a handful of others) in over a decade is the exception that proved the rule, and found it sound.

I have friends who don't read; who certainly wouldn't read fiction even if they were marooned in the Antarctic with a complete set of Penguins. What I always wonder about non-readers is: how do they get through the day? What do they have to look forward to?

For readers – utter readers, nutty readers, readin' fools – the daylight hours have no significance other than as a time of torment between the breakfast read and the bedtime return to the book. Days are wasted on trivial life matters, while the books pile up unread. Daylong we suffer, our longing broken only by the read on the way in, the read on the way home, the read at lunchtime and during the tea breaks, the read in the lav and the read in the van and the read under the desk and the read with the pen in the hand and the computer switched on in case anyone comes in. Other than that, the day is readless. But:

At school, at work, or in places worse than either, the hand-dragging slowness of the clock teases but does not kill us, because we know that if we just hold on then eventually, inevitably, we shall be horizontal and there will be black on white and there will be voices and pictures and the burning of fingerprint acid on fragrant paper. Readers are survivors;

that is the evolutionary purpose of reading. But non-readers: what do they have to look forward to? What gets them through the day? There must be times when, their minds empty of anything they have not personally seen or heard, they mistake the days for reality, and the world for something . . . complete.

There are three main types of non-reader. There are those who simply don't see the point of fiction, of things that are made up. These people often seem to lead perfectly happy, active, fulfilling and creative lives, entirely unaware that they are flawed. They can be amongst our most valuable citizens, not to be mocked, the holes in their hearts where the stories should be causing a great gravitational force which fills their hours with worthwhile activity. I still wonder what they do in the evenings, though. Sleep with the light on, perhaps?

Secondly there are the fundamentally uneducated; a self-explanatory sub-heading, and a group, deliberately created and maintained, without which liberal democracy could not exist.

Finally there are the overeducated, the largest of the non-reading subsets. You will never meet a graduate who loves reading, who lives to read, who when they tell her she's won the lottery jackpot says 'One more minute, all right? Just let me finish this chapter'.

We know that reading is an end in itself, that the point lies in the action not in the result, that the only books that should be read *because they should be read* are bus timetables. But the overeducated have been taught that reading is a duty, a chore, something to be got done.

And no sane man combines pleasure with duty. Why else do kings marry princesses, but sleep with horses?

What I mean to say is, if you're going to be a writer you have to be a reader first (and during, and afterwards). This is such a truism, that you may be wondering why I have mentioned it at all, let alone at such tedious length. The reason is that it isn't true. In fact, unnatural and unjust as this seems, I do know, or know of, several successful fiction writers who admit or even boast that they haven't read any fiction in years.

But – I have never met or heard of a successful fiction writer who hasn't been a mad keen reader at some time in his life. And that is what we must cling to.

It is perfectly true, and only natural, that editors give work to people they know; people they've given work to before, people they've met socially, and so on. Why shouldn't they? You do it yourself, with builders, plumbers and dentists. It's not a conspiracy aimed at keeping outsiders outside. It's just how things are. Naturally.

It is, undeniably, a great barrier to progress for writers who are just beginning. You can't get work without knowing an editor, and won't know an editor until you've worked for him. But, obviously, there are ways past the barrier – otherwise every single piece of writing in the world would be by one of a small group of old college mates. Whereas in actual fact, only about 98% of all the pieces of writing in the world . . .

Elsewhere in this book I discuss making First Contact with the inhabitants of the planet Editoria (the short version of which is 'Get an incredibly lucky break'). The important thing to realise is that once you've made that initial contact, you must hold onto it at all costs.

Once you're in with a particular editor, stay in; that relationship is the most valuable single advantage you can possibly have, far more valuable than talent, price competitiveness, or specialist knowledge.

Cherish every contact; claim your Christmas cards against income tax. Never throw away your old address books. For me this is easy; I am by nature the sort of person who sends Christmas cards to people I haven't seen for twenty years, or heard of in ten years. The way I look at it is, if they're dead, well, all I've wasted is the price of a stamp and a cheap charity greetings card. Whereas if they're not dead then probably all I've wasted is the price of a stamp and a cheap charity greetings card. I'm a letter writer by inclination. I'm the sort of person you were at primary school with and who you're still trying to shake off – moving house and changing your name every other month – as you approach your fortieth birthday. I'm someone you never had anything in common with in the first place, except that you once occupied the same vector in the time-space continuum. I'm a pain-in-the-arse nostalgic, and my address book is bigger than your house.

Make contact with people on the flimsiest excuse; not just editors you might be able to work for, but other writers who you admire (or have vaguely heard of). Drop them a line if you get a chance – providing further information concerning a topic they touched on in one of their columns, enclosing photocopied references if at all possible. You never know what will come of it. Most likely the people you harass in this way will emigrate, but apart from that you never know what will come of it.

At the very least, someone you once had correspondence with might, five years later, see a book of yours on a railway bookstand and pick it up, thinking '*Hmm*, I know that name'.

When my first book was published, I sent out a flyer to everyone I'd ever had any kind of contact with: readers who'd written to me, other writers with whom I'd corresponded, editors who knew me. Everyone. It obviously didn't work, since my first book sold about eleven copies globally, but that's not the point.

HOW TO BE BACKWARDS IN COMING FORWARD

Editors move around. Even if at the moment he's editor of something not very useful to you – you worked for him when he was at *The Jam Maker's Chronicle*, and now he's moved to *Golf Monthly* – don't lose touch. For all you know, ten years from now he might be the fiction editor at *Playboy*.

And this is always happening to me: I hear that an editor I once worked well with has got a new job, and this job is editing something that I would be ideally suited to write for, and yet my old pal hasn't been in touch.

It happened to me, for the last time I hope, just recently.

An editor who I knew thought highly of me had moved to the one job in the universe where he was most ideally placed to do me a bit of good, and after he'd been in post for two months, he still hadn't rung. 'Ah well,' I thought. 'He doesn't want me, he's gone off my stuff, he's forgotten I ever existed, or else now he's moving up in the world he doesn't think I'm good enough.'

But after a while I thought, *damn it*. I was going through a rather flat patch at the time, and so, abandoning dignity, coolness and any attempt at image-consciousness, I wrote to him: 'Congrats on your new job – got anything for me?'.

He phoned me as soon as he received my letter. Delighted to hear from me, was I really interested in writing for him? How wonderful! He would have been in touch himself, of course, but he just assumed I was too busy.

Too busy? Oh, yeah. It had been three weeks since I had last received a cheque, and that had been for thirty pounds. As far as I knew, my name hadn't appeared in print anywhere in the world during the last month, and I was so busy that I'd spent the whole of the previous day arranging the flowerpots in my garden shed in order of size (which wasn't as easy as it sounds, either; I do got both Imperial and Euro sizes in there, all mixed up, and some sizes – say 11C for instance – I do only got one of. How do you make a stack of one flowerpot?).

But of course, keeping track of my glorious career wasn't his job. While he might be one of a dozen editors who are constantly in my thoughts, for good or ill, I'm more likely to be one of fifty or sixty writers in his contacts book. He might have got round to me eventually, or he might not.

When I contacted him, he was genuinely pleased and probably relieved to hear from me – a freelance who he knew was reliable and was willing to do what he asked, that was one less assignment he had to worry about. And me? Ah, I was just glad to help an old pal. As always.

HOW I CAME TO BE BIG DOWN UNDER

For a time I was big down under. The greatest advantage of this, as you will readily understand, is that it gave me the right to use the 'big down under' joke, at will, forever after.

It happened like this. In 1979 I started work as a junior in the public library in Kentish Town. Already working there was another junior, named Alan. He and I became friends, and kept in touch after I'd moved to a different library. When Alan left the libraries to go and live in Australia (it's not easy to escape from the library service), we kept in touch. Years later, when I started doing a bit of broadcasting in London, I was amused and delighted to learn that Alan had already started doing a rather bigger bit of broadcasting in Sydney. After a while, Alan was producing his own radio show, needed someone to pop into the ABC's studios in Portland Place to record a book review, and . . . well, look, the point is, he *knew* me, right? Knew I'd done some radio, knew I was OK at it, knew what I could and couldn't do, knew what sort of books I could and couldn't talk about, knew what I sounded like, the sort of piece I was likely to write, what sort of job I'd make of reading it into a microphone. He knew me. It was only natural that he should ask me, instead of you, who he's never met in his life. That's how it works. It's not a conspiracy; it's just human nature. Over the next couple of years I did quite a number of broadcasts to Australia, on various subjects. The money wasn't bad, the work wasn't too hard, and anyway – who wouldn't want to be big down under, given the chance?

All right, there's a fair amount of coincidence involved in that story, and perhaps if I could be bothered I should rewrite it and put it in the *Luck* section instead. Perhaps I'll just put it there as well, instead of instead; pad the book out a bit, no one'll ever notice. But the point is, you don't have to be an Old Etonian to take advantage of an old boys' network. It's easier if you *are* one, of course, but assuming you're not, then you have to build your own network. And that means cherishing your contacts; never pass up the chance to bulk-buy cheap Christmas cards.

GET IN THERE, SON! My advice on joining things is simple: do it. Join every organisation you can find. If you're eligible to join a group – join it. If you're not eligible, join anyway if you think you can get away with it. Join, join, join.

Some of you, at this point, are curling your lips in what you imagine to be a superior sneer: there are many people who take pride in being non-joiners. It makes them more intellectual, they suppose, more independent. More cool.

Well, it doesn't, so there. All it does – if they're freelance writers – is cost them money.

You, I presume, like me, despise Jeffrey Archer. Still, I'm grateful to him, because it's thanks to Jeffrey Archer that I became a member of Equity, the actor's union.

His performance, for want of a better word, of one of his own novels on the radio, years ago, caused angry letters to appear in the columns of the sort of periodicals where angry letters appear. Wasn't he doing an actor out of a job, the angry letterists wanted to know; wasn't reading a serial on the wireless properly the business of an Equity member?

'No, ha ha, that's where you're wrong, hee hee, caught you with that one, didn't we,' replied the BBC. 'See, Mr Archer *is* a member of Equity. He qualified for membership when he had his own radio show for a while.' (Equity was then the last of the pre-entry closed shop unions.)

At that time, I was just starting to make a few broadcasts myself, and I thought – hmmm. An Equity card, eh? Could come in handy. So I applied, and I was accepted, and ever since, I've paid a small fee every year to remain a member in good standing.

It was a loophole, basically, which allowed someone who was patently not a thesp – *moi* – to gain that which many struggling in the stage profession would give their right hands for: the magic card. I think I've actually used the card only once – when I got a day's work as an extra in a pop video, and to my disappointment it turned out that the producer of that epic wasn't really bothered about such technicalities anyway – but you never know, you never know. One day that card could be worth money.

The one organisation you absolutely must join is The Writers' Guild of Great Britain. The WGGB (www.writersguild.org.uk) is the only TUC-affiliated trade union for writers – all writers, whether they work in books, film, TV, radio, theatre, or whatever. Not to belong to this body would be foolish, because there is likely to come a time when you need its help, as well as deeply ungrateful: it's the WGGB you have to thank for the standard contracts that publishers issue to authors, for the constantly renegotiated rates which TV and radio companies pay their scripters, and for more besides. If you're the sort of person who would happily work in an industry without joining the relevant union, then sod off. I forbid you from reading this book. Go away. Die.

When I joined the WGGB I automatically became a member of an obscure brotherhood known as the ALCS – The Authors' Licensing & Collecting Society Ltd. At least I think I did; I never really understood what the ALCS was all about, nor was I especially interested. But I filled in the forms anyway (listen to me now: *fill in every form you are sent*, no matter how boring or irrelevant it seems at the time), and years went by, as they will, and then one day I received a cheque, entirely unexpectedly, for a very odd, very precise amount of money, from ALCS. Apparently, one of my BBC radio stories had been re-broadcast in places like

Eire and Germany and heaven knows where else, and I was due a few shillings for each of these re-transmissions. And then there were some more shillings, something to do with a piece of writing on which I held copyright being photocopied in a public library in, I don't know, Zaire or somewhere.

I receive these cheques now a couple of times a year. They are rarely very large – totals of fifty quid, perhaps, or thereabouts, made up of little units like £5.81 and £10.88, although one year I got a cheque for almost a thousand pounds, and almost expired of shock and delight – but, by buggery, are they welcome! They always arrive, magically, just when I'm down to the last few pence of my agreed overdraft. And it *is* magic money – money seemingly plucked from the air, free money, the best kind of money there is.

It's important to realise that actually this is money (and the ALCS has collected many millions of pounds over the years) which you are owed, for work you have done; even if you didn't notice doing it at the time. And it's money which you would never be able to collect for yourself, because you wouldn't even know it was owing, unless you hired someone to listen to Belgian State Wireless for you on a full-time basis.

ALCS was established by, and is run by, writers working on behalf of writers. It is a wonderful organisation – in fact, I must make a note to send it a Christmas card this year, because there are few envelopes more welcome in the dull life of a writer than the ones that come from the mysterious, magical, munificent ALCS.

More free money can be had from Public Lending Right (PLR), the scheme that pays 'royalties' to authors when their books are borrowed from libraries. The main point to note about PLR is that it is the author's responsibility to register – your publisher or agent won't do it for you. So as soon as you have a book published, send off for the form and fill it in.

Genre organisations – whether readers' or writers' – are also worth your attention. I began my involvement with crime fiction by reviewing books for the now defunct *Million* magazine. That entitled me to become an associate member of the Crime Writers' Association, which entitled me to submit stories to the CWA's annual anthologies. My first ever published crime story was shortlisted for the CWA's Dagger Award, and its publication led directly to me selling numerous short stories since then to magazines and anthologies in Britain and abroad.

Abroad: if you're eligible for membership of the CWA, you're probably also eligible to join Mystery Writers of America. And so on. There are dozens of organisations, small and large, domestic, foreign and international, and I seriously advise you to join as many as possible, for market information, selling opportunities, professional protection, useful contacts, and solidarity. (The British Fantasy Society and the British Science Fiction Association, in particular, produce superb newsletters.)

Of course, if you like, you can be a cool, sophisticated, non-joining loner.

Or you can make a few bob. Up to you, pal, entirely up to you.

HOW TO GET YOUR HEAD SNAPPED

At one stage in the lurching tragicomedy which we playfully refer to as my 'writing career' I had several photo-topped magazine columns on the go at once, and it befell me one day to be travelling on the Tube when I saw someone reading a magazine.

Naturally, if you work in magazines you can't help looking. I was strap-dangling, enjoying the familiar sensation of stale grease and sharp rust penetrating my palm, and the reader was sitting down. I peeped over his shoulder and saw that, sure enough, he was reading a column with a photo of me at the top. Cor, eh? This had never happened to me before.

And he was nodding. He'd read a few lines, then he'd nod. Then he'd read a few more lines and then he'd nod again. Occasionally he'd grunt, perhaps because he'd read somewhere that too much nodding can give you passive smoking.

I was pretty seriously coming round to the idea of tapping him on the shoulder and saying 'Here, you see that piccy? That's I, that is' when the nodding man gave a final nod and a final grunt and tore the magazine into four pieces, spat on each piece four times, and hurled them onto the floor with a barking cry of 'TOSSER!'.

His hands were all hair and knuckle. All hair and knuckle. I took off my specs and combed my fringe forward over my face. I got off at the next stop and caught a bus instead.

If you're lucky, one day you're going to have your photograph taken for publication. ('If you're lucky' because, remember, all this is what you want, so you've no one to blame but yourself when it turns out to be hateful.)

It's not a big part of the freelance writer's life, being snapped, but it's one worth thinking about for a while; it's one worth having a strategy for, decided in advance.

Some people really hate being photographed, and writers are more likely to suffer such phobias, I would guess, than the average citizen. I don't, of course, for I am unnaturally handsome, with an inch-perfect body and an ever-ready smile – but supposing I wasn't? Suppose I was just some ordinary human, like you? What part of having my picture took would give me the night sweats?

First to come to mind is the fear that one will look like a total arse. Or even worse, an incomplete arse; a bit or lump of arse, inaccurately sliced and unconvincingly stuck upon a pole to stand as deputy for a human face. Cor, imagine looking like that.

This I'm afraid is inevitable. Go to a public library and look through all the periodicals on the racks: you won't find one contributor's photo that doesn't resemble either an arse or a section of arse. (Or Cliff Richard; for some reason, a lot of column-top photographs look like Cliff Richard. Could this be something to do with the fact that many such pictures depict young persons, immortalised in c.1963?)

In other words, it's not worth worrying about how awful you look in your published pictures, because you *will* look awful. So instead, concentrate on matters over which you have some control.

For instance, a question which affects a high proportion of us: specs on or off? I first became intimate with the zoom lens during one of my earliest regular-money jobs, freelancing for the *London Evening Standard* during the mid-80s. Once or twice a week, I would be sent out to do something uncomfortable – riding a water bike, or jiving with a troupe of lindyhoppers – accompanied by a photographer. In those days I wore glasses which automatically became sunglasses in bright light. Unfortunately, these bins had a side effect unknown to me or to the photographer: in photos they appeared completely shaded, so that the earliest pictures of me showed someone with no visible eyes at all. I looked like a terrorist. Mr Carlos the Jackal, to be precise.

The obvious solution was to remove the specs, but this led to another, perhaps more predictable problem: I couldn't see anything. I now appeared in the paper each week staring myopically into the distance, and more often than not staring in the opposite direction to whatever it was I was supposed to be studying. The effect was profoundly disconcerting. Folk began to accuse me to my face of irony or surrealism; of *undermining the conventions of the form*.

Eventually, the *Standard* came up with an answer to the problem. They stopped taking my picture, and got me to compile the What's On column instead. This was not a promotion.

The specs-off option, however, does have one advantage which for me tips the balance in its favour. If you're not wearing your glasses, you don't look like you, and this lessens the likelihood of someone recognising you in a pub or on a train and engaging you in debate about something you've written. Until this has actually happened to you, you can probably not imagine just how undesirable an event it is. Take my word for it; and if you don't habitually wear glasses, buy yourself a pair, along with a false beard perhaps, for use in a photographic context.

My first column-top photo was for a consumer magazine with a largely female readership. We need a pic, the editor told me. Have you got something suitable? I sent in a few from the family album, but they were rejected: 'These are no good, they make you look like a segment of Cliff Richard's botty'. And so a session with a professional photographer was arranged.

He arrived at my flat rather early one morning; photographers evidently keep different hours from writers, and imagine, wrongly, that their subjects are capable of looking human before lunch. Being new to all this, I'd thought the process would take fifteen minutes, maybe half an hour if the snapper was a perfectionist, and that I would then be free to drag my hangover round to the pub for some medical attention.

It took him half an hour just to unpack his gear from the car.

Another hour was spent setting up lights on tripods, and backcloths and reflectors and various other bits of kit, until my living-room looked like the operating theatre from M*A*S*H.

We then broke for a cup of coffee, after which he spent at least an hour photographing my head from every angle. The poor man obviously took pride in his craft, and was desperate to find some means of presenting me to my public in a way which might cause as little offence as possible. That he failed (the published picture made me look like an arse with a hangover) does not suggest any lack of skill on his part; rather it speaks eloquently of the nervous tension which grew in me throughout that distressing morning, and which is captured, in the finished product, in my pale face, my blood-blancmange eyes, and the stretched-to-breaking-point jaw muscles clearly visible beneath my skin.

'You could smile if you like,' he suggested at one point. 'Might help.'

'I *ang* skiling,' I replied.

'Oh right,' he said. 'Sure, looks terrific. Just one more roll of film, perhaps . . .'

Next time I was called up for posing duty – another mag, another column-top shot – I went prepared. I arrived at the magazine's West End offices early, and equipped with mineral water, a crossword puzzle, some of those 'banana' things that tennis players are so fond of, and a hipflask of relaxant brandy. I'd had a good night's sleep, and spent the tube journey into London doing face-pulling exercises to bring some movement and colour into my features.

'I'm here for my portrait session,' I told the editor. 'Has the camera team arrived yet?'

'Ah, right,' said the editor. He turned to yell over his shoulder at the office junior. 'Jim! Did you remember to bring your mum's camera in with you? Good lad – just take this guy outside and shoot him for me, will you?'

Jim took me outside, leant me against a wall (I could feel that my face was mostly in shadow, but I didn't mention it to Jim; for all I knew, those had been the editor's precise instructions) and took my pic. Then – because he was obviously an ambitious boy, with no lack of initiative – he took it again, 'Just in case the first one don't come out. Me mum says this film's a bit past its sell-by date'.

I looked like an arse in that one too. But at least it was quick.

If I had my choice, I would quite happily go the rest of my life without ever again seeing my face – or anything resembling my face – reproduced in print. Believe me, it's a thrill which quickly palls. But choice doesn't come into it, and people continue to ask me for photos. It's no good wondering why: it is the custom that a columnist should be pictured at the top of his column, and that's that. Readers like it, apparently – though only, one suspects, from motives of cruelty and a desire to feel superior to the writer – and it is, in a sense, an honour; at least, a piece of writing which carries a photo is clearly defined as a column, and not as a mere feature or article.

These days, I eschew professional lensmen, and instead stock up every five years or so with a roll or two of informal, but in focus, black and white snaps, which my brother-in-law takes after we've both had a few beers.

In half I wear my glasses and in half I take them off; in half I'm bearded, in half I'm shaved (in that order, obviously). I pose for these sessions in the garden, so that a generous reader might attribute any extreme signs of weirdness to the effects on human flesh of global warming or a passing hurricane.

Out of thirty-six exposures I can usually select three or four which seem unlikely to constitute a felony in any country with a secular government.

I use these for column-tops, but also as souvenirs for my 'fans'. Because, extraordinary as it might sound, I have occasionally had readers writing to me care of this magazine or that and asking for a signed photograph. In such cases I am careful to select one of my least recognisable false-beard jobs, and to reply from an address that begins 'PO Box 100, Alaska'.

I mean, no offence, but you know – someone writing in for a signed photo of a magazine columnist? You've got to wonder, haven't you, just exactly what sort of oddo would spend a stamp to satisfy so bizarre a lust.

HOW TO GET KILLED

Replying to correspondence from your readers is something you will have to deal with sooner than you might expect; it isn't only Terry Pratchett who gets letters from fans. There are many kinds of readers' letters; these are a few of them:

> **1**. The Fuck Off And Die. I get a fair number of these, but then, that's only fair, because I send a fair number of them, too. They usually come from religious believers, feminists, or anybody else who seeks an end to world violence.

2. The Sensible Hate Mail. These are sensible in the sense that they often involve complete words, or even sentences, and are rarely written in pig's blood. They come from all sorts of outraged people, except religious believers and feminists. Defenders of astrology are notorious for sending this type of letter.

3. The Total Bonkers Stuff. This breaks down further into two clear subsets.
a: Nutty But Friendly. In my experience these come from men, and are densely-written, barely legible, and scarcely punctuated. It soon becomes clear that the fact that the writer has written to you, as opposed to anybody else, is insignificant. He is talking to himself; his argument makes sense only to himself. He just happened to see your name in print, and that's why you've got the letter this week instead of, say, Barry Took or Helmut Kohl.
b: Nutty And Nasty. Written by women (again, this is in my experience; it may be that Nasty Nut women write to men and vice versa). Very long letters, often periodically comprehensible, in which you, the recipient, are held responsible, as it were archetypically, for all the sufferings of the correspondent and the world.

4. The Information Sought And Found Department. 'In your column last week you mentioned a sweet called Nob-Lickers and wondered if they were still available. You may be interested to know that Nob-Lickers are indeed still available at a shop in Melton Mowbray called . . .' *or* '. . . mentioned in your column last week that, at the time when the Martians kidnapped you, you were cooking a vegetarian version of sheep's eyes. I am married to a Vegetarian Bedouin, and would be very interested to know . . .'

5. Actual Fan Mail. This isn't as rare as you might suppose, and can be very cheering on a dark day. Some fan letters congratulate you for holding similar opinions to those of the letter-writer, others express gratitude for laughter, or general appreciation of one's overall niceness and reliability. A few stick in the mind individually. The most letters I have ever had in one go (of all the types mentioned above, though coming out roughly 50/50 for and against) came after I wrote a piece for a Sunday paper condemning the existence of religious broadcasting. My favourite came from a woman who was very ill in hospital. She had clearly taken great pleasure from my article (if you'll pardon the expression, Vicar), largely because during her stay on the ward she had been haunted by a pious acquaintance who insisted on visiting her and enlightening her on the fascinating subject of God's will.

The second largest amount of mail I have ever received came after I wrote a paragraph in a diary column complaining that I was unable to purchase small weights to prevent my net curtains lifting in the breeze. Which just goes to show. Something.

I am strongly of the opinion that replying to readers' letters is an inescapable duty, part of the *noblesse oblige* of freelancing. It is also a bloody good way of getting useable material for nuffink. Countless are the times I have filled whole columns with stuff from readers' correspondence; in other words, I have been paid while others have done the writing. I have made valued acquaintanceships, even friendships, from correspondence with readers (and as a reader, from correspondence with writers).

But more importantly, if someone can be bothered to write to you, you must be bothered to write back. Editors, and a distressing proportion of writers, despise their readers (viewers, listeners and so on). I've seen sad readers' letters passed around media offices for a giggle, or pinned up on the corkboard in the coffee room.

My rule is to reply to any letter which carries a return address. To offensive letters I reply offensively, to bland letters I reply blandly, to requests for recipes I reply mischievously ('Next, add the six buckets of gooseberries to the curry paste, stirring all the while to prevent sticking') if I'm hungover.

My only two exceptions are that I never reply to a letter or phone message from an employee of Rupert Murdoch's newspapers (due to the trade union boycott which is still in force) and I reserve the right to end a correspondence with Nutty Nasty Women (as detailed above) after, say, six or seven letters. After all, I'm not *made* of time.

If you find hate mail upsetting, then you could ignore it, or report it to the police (there have been some interesting legal precedents in this area lately), or, best of all, get another job. All other categories deserve at least a brief reply.

I've been a writer of fan letters all my life. I have a clear mental record of those people who have and haven't written back, and every now and then I go into a chain bookstore, turn to page 21 of the non-respondents' latest books, and write there the word BUTTOCKS in green ink. Because my view is, if you can't be bothered to write, don't become a writer.

Afterword

This is not intended to be an inspirational book. If anything, I mean it to be *dis*inspirational. But I would be dishonest, and fashionably cynical, if I tried to pretend that there wasn't, every now and then, a day when I've gone to bed thinking 'Well, that was a good day's work; that was worth getting up for this morning'.

On the day that an aeroplane crashed on Lockerbie, I watched the TV news like millions of others, and, like millions of others, became increasingly horrified (I've chosen that word carefully) by the ignorance, incompetence, irrelevance and insensitivity of the reporters and editors covering the 'story'; by the sheer joy that the disaster industry evidently took in that awfulness; by the sight of politicians wandering the ruins, getting in people's way – while the rescue workers searched for bodies, the politicians searched for votes. And while politicians canvassed the dead, journalists picked amid the rubble, searching for awards to put on their mantelpieces.

I felt I had to write something about it. Writing can, as we all know, be a way of releasing pain and frustration; for some reason, writing things down seems to take some of the steam out of you, and leave you better able to carry on with your life.

But still I was shy of the job. I knew it would be a massive undertaking, if I was to do it right, and suppose I wrote it but then couldn't get it published? No, I couldn't face it. Even so, I videotaped all that night's news programmes.

The next morning, the editor of *Midweek* magazine rang, to ask if I'd watched last night's news, and wasn't it disgusting, and why didn't I write something about the bastards?

So I did. And it *was* a huge job. I probably wrote ten thousand words that day, all of them angry and venomous and despairing. Somehow all that had to be cut down to a few pages of rational argument – and it had to be done quickly. I've rarely worked so hard on anything. There were times when I felt as if I really was sweating blood; it's no coincidence that clichés come alive at times of stress.

The finished article kept getting longer. Every couple of hours I'd ring the editor and ask him if I could have another 400 words, and he would say, 'Go on, write what needs to be written'. Eventually it was finished, and *Midweek* (not a serious political weekly, but a light-hearted commuter's mag, which makes this all the more remarkable) printed it as the cover story on the following issue.

It was a bloody good piece. Years later, people still mention it to me. I've never forgotten it: even now, I could probably recite it to you word for word, not because I've read it so often – I haven't – but because I wrote it *so damn hard* that every word is hot-metalled onto my memory.

I got letters and phone calls from people I hadn't heard from in years, and from people I'd never heard of before, all saying the one thing that every writer most longs to hear: that I had said exactly what they had wanted to say. It was one of the best jobs of work I have ever done in my life, and I am enormously proud of it. I'd be quite happy to have that piece carved on my tombstone, except that it's several thousand words long.

Anyway, I just thought I'd mention that before I go. Sometimes, it really is worth being a freelance writer. Usually, when it's raining and there's a Tube strike.

Interzone
FOR 22 YEARS AND COUNTING ONE OF THE WORD'S
LEADING SCIENCE FICTION AND FANTASY MAGAZINES

The 3rd Alternative
EXTRAORDINARY NEW FICTION, ART, INTERVIEWS,
REVIEWS, CINEMA, COMICS, COMMENTARY

Crimewave
WIDELY RECOGNISED AS THE WORLD'S BEST, AND
BEST-LOOKING, CRIME FICTION MAGAZINE

The Fix
INVALUABLE FOR THE CREATIVE WRITER AND READER

American Graveyards by Ray Nayler
A DEBUT NOVEL DESCRIBED BY BLUE MURDER AS
'DARK, DANGEROUS AND INTOXICATING'

The Planet Suite by Allen Ashley
A COSMIC AND SPIRITUAL TOUR THROUGH THE
SOLAR SYSTEM, YEARS AHEAD OF ITS TIME

www.ttapress.com